For Grant Harmon
December 1992

mitte hamum
et eum piscem qui primus ascenderit
tolle.

Mt. 17:26 (NRSV Mt. 17:27)

Frank

FLY FISHING

for

SMALLMOUTH BASS

FLY FISHING
for
SMALLMOUTH
BASS

Harry Murray

Illustrations by Dave Whitlock

Nick Lyons Books

LYONS & BURFORD, *PUBLISHERS*

Printed in the United States of America

10 9 8 7 6 5 4 3

Library of Congress Cataloging-in-Publication Data

Murray, Harry.
    Fly fishing for smallmouth bass.

    Includes index.
    1. Smallmouth bass fishing. 2. Fly fishing.
I. Title.
SH681.M87 1989   799.1′758   89-8050
ISBN 0-941130-85-1

Contents

Preface

Fly fishing for smallmouth bass has somehow been misplaced between high-speed bassboats and trout stream entomology. As an advanced form of angling it has been almost ignored in recent years. Harry Murray puts it in perspective.

Black bass tournaments for both smallmouths and largemouths have shunted the fly rod into the background. It doesn't go very well in competition fishing on large reservoirs and somehow hasn't adapted well to the terms ''sows'' and ''hawgs'' as favored by the modern faithful. Most black bass writers have stopped their fly rod coverage with descriptions of how to make a loud pop with a surface bug. And one thick hardcover text that purports to cover all bass fishing methods does not even mention the fly rod. All this time trout fishing has been covered in extreme detail and occasionally almost to absurdity. There is a place for Murray's book.

Murray has the ideal background for his subject. He is an angling instructor and lecturer, a guide, a master fly tyer and a tireless angler who experiments on the good days as well as the bad. He owns a tackle shop. He has another special qualification as one of the best of technical trout fishermen and has brought some of the finer points of trout angling to bass fishing, something it badly needs. There is more to the fly rod for bass than loud pops along the bank.

He goes into detail seldom found in anything on bass fishing and does it especially with underwater streamers and nymphs. This is new ground for most black bass flyrodders, who may think the technique of fishing wet for bass is simply throwing something that sinks and dragging it in. Now he goes into leaders specially tied for special jobs, shows how the various sinking lines and line tips will work at different depths and describes what deep-going nymphs and streamers are doing down there with various line actions and, above all, with various current actions. Suddenly all of this becomes very important to casters who haven't thought much about it before. He goes into the various bass patterns and illustrates the whole works.

He doesn't have much modern competition in this area. If you want more detail you'll have to wait for new techniques to be developed.

It is difficult to fish side-by-side with Harry Murray without watching him out of the corner of your eye. There's the feeling that if you don't catch him at it you may miss something he forgot to tell you about smallmouth bass and flyrods. The audiences at his lectures are almost worshipful and his students tend to be wide-eyed.

Maybe the best thing about Murray is that he really wants everybody to catch fish—as long as they put most of them back.

CHARLES F. WATERMAN

Introduction

The smallmouth bass is the gentleman of the warm water fish. For me, the best way to angle for this worthy adversary is by fly fishing.

The natural foods the smallmouth feeds upon can be successfully duplicated with flies and bugs, their actions imparted very convincingly with fly tackle. The fly fishing tactics we use for him are easy to learn and highly productive. Most of all, fly fishing for smallmouth bass is just a lot of fun.

After hearing me describe some of the techniques I use on smallmouth a knowledgeable angler once ventured that I was really "trout fishing for bass." He was only partly right. True, some of the tactics I use on the large streams in the Rockies for large browns and rainbows are similar to those I use on smallmouth, but smallmouth tactics go beyond that. And we are not just gearing down largemouth bass tactics for his smallmouth cousin.

Certainly we draw upon the various ways of angling for these other fish, even reaching out to borrow some things from the bonefish angler, but we do not stop there.

The smallmouth demands a customized blend of all the angling tactics, know-how, insight, and understanding an angler can draw upon. Consistent success, especially for the larger smallmouth, comes from an understanding of just how he will be feeding under various conditions, the water in which he will be located, and how successfully you use various techniques and specific flies in those situations.

I will cover all of this in the following pages. I will discuss the most consistent angling methods as well as some that are specialized. Most of these techniques result from years of my own trial and error and I hope you will be able to learn from things that have come to me the hard way. If our hindsight were as good as our foresight we would catch more fish by a darned sight!

Rods, reels, lines and all other basic tackle will be covered as they apply to the smallmouth, with special attention given to customized leaders, which are a great help in fishing underwater flies.

The smallmouth's natural foods will be discussed with respect to where they are located, their behavior, and the flies that match them. I will also survey how to read a river so you can blend this understanding of the foods with a working knowledge of the smallmouth's environment.

Finally we will investigate the fishing techniques and tactics most successful on smallmouth waters. The discussion of top-water fishing will include the best ways to fish some old reliable popper and hair patterns on both streams and lakes; it then expands to cover some highly successful, but little known, procedures.

We will cover a broad variety of streamer-fishing tactics in all types of waters, at all times of the year. Here we will cover some special techniques for big fish.

You will come to have a complete understanding of smallmouth nymphing tactics, learning how to fish nymphs right on the stream bottom with complete control of the drift. Special techniques for strike detection, a key component of this type of fishing, are broken down step by step.

Basic fly pattern concepts will be covered in great detail, enabling you to evaluate existing patterns for their use under specific situations. These concepts will also help you to design and tie productive flies for any type of water or stream condition. With this basic information we will go into the actual tying of many of the most productive smallmouth flies and bugs.

I have tried to present this book as a series of building blocks which you can add to your present skills and improve your smallmouth game. I also urge you to go beyond this text to examine your home waters, the fish, their foods, and their feeding habits to develop and improve additional tactics—not just to catch more smallmouth but to enhance the many rewards they can give.

1

Smallmouth Fly-Fishing Tackle

Rods

The most popular fly rods for smallmouth angling are from 8½ to 9½ feet long and carry size 6, 7, or 8 fly lines. These can be constructed of bamboo, fiberglass, graphite, boron, or boron-graphite blends. The last three materials are preferred because they have the power needed to cast heavy bass bugs while remaining relatively lightweight.

In my smallmouth fly-fishing schools I have encountered students with fly rods possessing a broad variety of actions. Only those with very delicate tips cause a lot of trouble; such rods work fine with small trout flies, but are disappointing when one tries to cast large, wind-resistant bass bugs or heavily weighted streamers.

If you already own a fly rod for a number 6, 7, or 8 line feel free to use it for your initial smallmouth fishing. If you plan to purchase a fly rod specifically for smallmouth fishing I recommend one of the new graphite rods with a strong tip and a relatively slow butt which are made especially for bass fishing. The strong tips of these rods are a great help in lifting large bass bugs from the water surface and the soft butts provide a slower casting cycle. This type of action is very pleasant to use and affords excellent line control for accurate bug casting.

Early in the season I like to use a rod that handles a size 8 line. At this time of the year it is often necessary to use heavily weighted nymphs and streamers to reach the smallmouth holding close to the stream bottom; an eight-weight outfit is a great help when casting these weighted flies.

As the waters warm in late spring the smallmouth starts to take surface bugs. I still stick with an eight-weight outfit here, because at this time of the year I am usually throwing fairly large surface bugs. Keep in mind that the air resistance

1

of surface bugs can present problems when trying to cast too large a bug with too small an outfit. There is much to be said for the ''big bugs for big bass'' theory—especially when rivers maintain a good water level.

I usually stick with an eight-weight outfit until the streams get low in mid to late summer, when I switch over to a six-weight, the lighter line being less likely to scare the bass as it settles on the water surface. From mid-summer until fall there are good catches to be had without using large flies; these smaller patterns are easy to cast on a six-weight outfit.

Smallmouth bass fly-fishing tackle. Photo courtesy The Orvis Company.

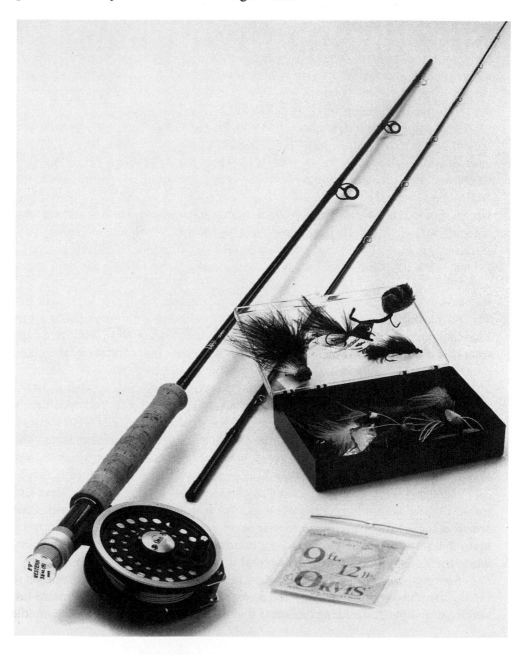

REELS

Fly reels for bass fishing should be durable, lightweight models. I find that I am much harder on smallmouth reels than I am on trout reels, even on waters of equivalent size. I don't know why this should be, it just is. Although I want a strong reel I do not want it to be excessively heavy.

Aluminum and other lightweight materials used in today's reels allow models which will hold the full fly line with 150 feet of backing and still weigh less than six ounces. Some, in fact, weigh only four ounces.

Most smallmouth anglers prefer single-action reels but a few like multiplying reels. Single-action reels recover one full wrap of line onto the reel spool with each complete turn of the reel handle; multiplying reels retrieve two or more wraps of line with each turn of the reel handle. The choice between these is a matter of personal preference: you will be gaining some extra weight by selecting the multiplying style, but it is not excessive.

A few anglers use automatic fly reels. By pressing a lever on this reel with the small finger of the rod hand it is possible to recover a great amount of line very quickly, which can be very helpful when fishing from a canoe or boat. Automatic reels are heavier than manual reels and are fading rapidly in popularity. One great advantage of the manual reels over the automatics is the ease with which spools can be changed. I like to carry two extra spools for each of my reels so I can quickly change to the specific floating, sink tip, or sinking-head fly line I might need.

LINES

Fly lines are a crucial part of our smallmouth tackle and although we do not require a broad selection, a few basic styles can expand our horizons.

The basic fly line is a floating model which can be constructed with either a conventional weight-forward taper (usually preferred when distance casting) or with a special bass bug weight-forward taper. The bass bug fly lines have a heavier, shorter front taper than the regular weight-forward lines. They are specially designed for casting large, wind-resistant bass bugs, heavy nymphs, and streamers. I especially like the bass bug taper lines for fishing nymphs on a short line.

Another useful fly line for smallmouth is the sinking-tip fly line. The first ten feet of the sinking-tip line sinks while the rest of the line floats. These lines are great for fishing nymphs and streamers on the bottom in moderately fast water up to five feet deep, and in lakes. The sinking portion pulls the fly to the bottom, while the floating portion makes for good drift control and strike detection.

Sinking-tip lines are built with several different sinking rates. In order to distinguish the various lines they are often referred to as fast sinking, extra-fast sinking and super-fast sinking models. I find the extra-fast sinking tip—the middle

bass

one, with a sink rate of 2.50 to 4.25 inches per second—about right for small-mouth fishing.

In a few situations I find a thirty-foot, extra-fast sinking head to be helpful. This usually happens in early spring when the streams are especially full or when I have to reach extra depth in lakes.

When trying to decide just which sinking-tip or sinking-head line to use in a specific stream remember that the speed of the current, as well as the depth of the stream, must be considered. There are areas within many good smallmouth streams where strong runs and shoots only three or four feet deep hold good fish that can be very tough to reach with a fly. These are often runs jammed up so close beneath heavy riffles that it is impossible to cast far enough upstream to give the flies time to sink as they approach the hotspot. In such a situation I like to use the fastest sinking-tip line that I have with a leader not over six feet long.

LEADERS

Leaders are probably the most neglected part of the smallmouth fly fisherman's tackle. Understanding the correct leaders to use in specific situations can be a great help in assuring consistent success.

The basic leader for floating lines is about nine feet long, either knotted or knotless styles. I prefer the knotted style, but if aquatic weeds are present the knotless style will prevent grass from collecting on the leader.

Smooth casting and presentation requires that the stiffness of the leader butt match the stiffness of the tip section of the fly line. For most good leader material this means using about .021-inch diameter to match most fly lines used in the smallmouth sizes (roughly 6-, 7-, and 8-weight lines). Keep in mind that this .021 inch is only an expression of diameter, not stiffness—if you are using a fairly flexible material you will want to use a larger size and if your leader material is very stiff you should step down to about .019 or .017 for the leader butt. It would be helpful if the manufacturers of leader material would adopt a uniform system of labeling all of their material with a flexibility rating as well as diameter and strength, but until they do the angler will have to keep his wits about him and remember that flexibility varies from one make of leader to another.

While the flexibility of the leader butt is important for smooth casting, the flexibility of the tippet is the most important aspect influencing the natural drift of flies and bugs. It is imperative that we select the proper leader for the size and weight fly we plan to fish, either by adding a complete leader for the job at hand or by reworking the one already attached to the fly line. The key here is the tippet; it must be stiff enough to turn over the fly and yet flexible enough to permit the fly to be manipulated in a convincing manner.

An example: fishing a weighted size-4 sculpin streamer in the full streams of spring we need a leader with a tippet of OX, whereas fishing a size-10 popper to spooky fish in low water during September requires a 3X tippet. If we used a

3X tippet on the big streamer it simply would not cast smoothly and may even fail to turn over the fly. Using the heavy OX tippet on our small popper in low water conditions would not bring as many strikes as a finer tippet would.

Both the weight and the bulk of the flies and bugs must be considered in leader selection. Heavily weighted size 2 and 4 underwater flies and bulky size 2 and 4 surface bugs are best cast on a leader no finer than OX. We can drop on down to 1X, 2X, and 3X as we use progressively smaller flies; on rare occassions I will even drop down to 4X when using size 10 or 12 flies late in the summer as the streams get low.

I do not find that it is often necessary to go as fine as a 4X tippet. I definitely improve my success, however, both in numbers as well as size of bass, by going to a twelve-foot leader for late summer and early fall fishing. I have spooked many nice smallmouth in low water conditions by using a leader so short that it permitted the fly line to come within their view; a twelve-foot leader helps overcome this problem.

The leader can be constructed to help detect strikes with nymphs and streamers. For the past fifteen years I have been building my leaders with fluorescent monofilament for the three butt sections. I used to dye my own, but now there is some available already dyed fluorescent red under the name Amnesia. This casts very well and is highly visible to the fisherman in the water.

In addition to this bright butt leader I use one or two indicators on my leaders to aid in strike detection with all underwater flies. My favorites are the Scientific Anglers indicators. These are easy to install on the leader, highly visible in the water, and do not interfere with smooth casting. I like to have one of these indicators at the line-leader junction (one of Dave Whitlock's tricks) and one about four feet up the leader from the fly; often I even add a third indicator about half way between the other two. This leader rig—the fluorescent butt sections with two or three indicators—is what I call my "strike detection system." In the fifteen or so years I've been using this it has never let me down. It has also been the single most helpful item in aiding many of the students in my bass fly-fishing schools to move from so-so nymph fishermen to very proficient anglers in a short time. They simply cannot believe the help in strike detection this leader rig provides!

Leaders for sinking lines should seldom be over six feet long. If they are, we defeat ourselves by negating the purpose of these special lines. Sinking fly lines enable us to fish our flies close to the bottom by first sinking themselves, then pulling the leader down with them which in turn pulls down the fly. If the leader is too long it allows the fly to ride too high in the water.

Sometimes a longer leader (eight to ten feet) can be used with a sinking-tip line with a floating or shallow-running bug to achieve a diving effect. When stripped the sinking tip line pulls the bug under the surface, and when we pause the bug rises back to the surface.

There are also special leaders that are basically floating leaders which, with

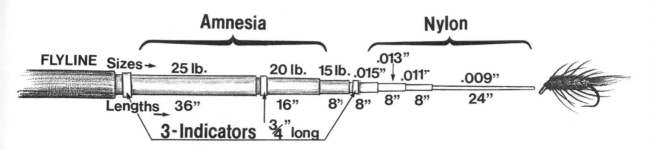

BRIGHT BUTT LEADER.

the addition of various sinking, high-density line sections along the leader, help get flies to the bottom. These are easy to use and to adapt to a variety of situations on the stream, since the various sections of the leaders have loop-to-loop connections.

Some ready-made leaders are constructed with blood knots that have lead sections built into them at various locations. These too are helpful in sinking flies. I find those with the sinking portion only two to four feet behind the fly do a better job than those with the weight built into the butt section. However, how much this type of leader will help varies with the fishing situation, so it is wise to experiment.

Another trick that helps get underwater flies to the bottom is something I picked up long ago from a steelhead angler. At that time when one thought about getting flies to the bottom quickly he used a lead-core head. It was a natural step from these full sinking thirty-foot heads to what, at that time, we called ''lead-core mini heads.'' There are now many excellent fast-sinking lines on the market so it is no longer necessary to limit the construction of these ''mini sinking heads'' to lead-core lines.

I construct these mini sinking heads in a variety of lengths from six inches to two feet long out of sinking lines of various densities. I build loops on each end of these line sections by folding about a one-inch section back on itself and whip finishing a knot over it. I then coat this with Pliobond.

I carry an assortment of these mini sinking heads in my fishing vest and install them into my leader when I need extra depth. For example, if I am using a nine-foot, 2X leader with a floating line and want to get my streamer deeper I will cut this leader about three feet above the fly and tie a double surgeon's loop on both of the exposed end pieces. I will then simply attach my mini sinking head to these pieces with a loop-to-loop connection. The entire operation takes about one minute and it is not even necessary to remove the fly while doing it. You end up with a nine-foot leader with a fast sinking section out close to the fly. This mini sinking head casts much better than a split shot work-up of the same sink rate and does not hang on the bottom as quickly.

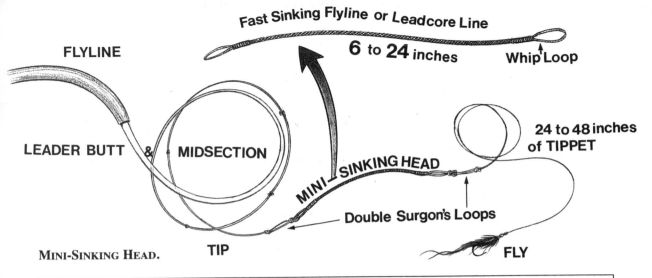

FLYLINE

Fast Sinking Flyline or Leadcore Line

6 to 24 inches

Whip Loop

LEADER BUTT & MIDSECTION

MINI-SINKING HEAD

24 to 48 inches of TIPPET

Double Surgon's Loops

MINI-SINKING HEAD.

TIP

FLY

SMALLMOUTH BASS LEADERS
(Length & Diameter Expressed in Inches)

Leaders for Low Water Conditions

12-ft, 0X		12-ft, 1X		12-ft, 2X		12-ft, 3X		12-ft, 4X	
Diameter	Length	Diameter	Length	Diameter	Length	Diameter	Length	Diameter	Length
.021	48	.021	48	.021	48	.021	48	.021	48
.019	36	.019	36	.019	36	.019	36	.019	36
.017	20	.017	18	.017	18	.017	12	.017	12
.015	8	.015	6	.015	6	.015	6	.015	6
.013	8	.013	6	.013	6	.013	6	.013	6
.011	24	.011	6	.011	6	.011	6	.011	6
		.010	24	.009	24	.009	6	.009	6
						.008	24	.008	24

Leaders for Normal Conditions

9-ft, 0X		9-ft, 1X		9-ft, 2X		9-ft, 3X		9-ft, 4X	
Diameter	Length	Diameter	Length	Diameter	Length	Diameter	Length	Diameter	Length
.021	40	.021	36	.021	36	.021	36	.021	36
.019	20	.019	16	.019	16	.019	18	.019	18
.017	8	.017	8	.017	8	.017	6	.017	6
.015	8	.015	8	.015	8	.015	6	.015	6
.013	8	.013	8	.013	8	.013	6	.013	6
.011	24	.011	8	.011	8	.011	6	.011	6
		.010	24	.009	24	.009	6	.009	6
						.008	24	.007	24

Leaders for Sinking Lines

6-ft, 0X		6-ft, 1X		6-ft, 2X	
Diameter	Length	Diameter	Length	Diameter	Length
.019	36	.019	30	.019	30
.017	12	.017	12	.017	12
.015	6	.015	6	.015	6
.013	6	.013	6	.013	6
.011	12	.011	6	.011	6
		.010	12	.009	12

KNOTS

Knots are as important to the smallmouth angler as any other fisherman. From the broad selection of fishing knots, the smallmouth fisherman can rely on a relatively small number of dependable stand-bys.

      The needle knot is the surest method of attaching line to leader and an offshot of this, the nail knot, is ideal for attaching line to backing. The blood knot is the standard for leader construction. The double surgeon's loop is very strong and ideal anywhere a loop is needed. The Duncan loop is excellent for attaching all ring-eyed flies and bugs to the leader. My favorite knot for attaching all up- or down-eyed flies to the leader is the Spence Turle.

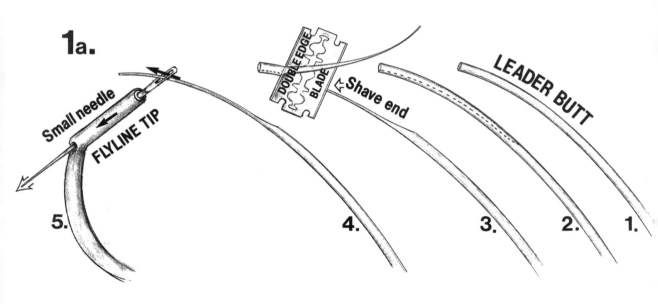

NEEDLE KNOT. *(For use with knotted leaders.)*

Step 1A

1, 2, & 3: Using a razor blade, shave the last two inches of the butt of a knotted leader to a fine point.

4: Insert this point into the eye of a small needle that has been inserted into the end of the fly line. The tip of the needle should stick out through the side of the line one-fourth of an inch from the end of the line.

5: Being careful to allow at least one-half inch of leader to extend beyond the eye of the needle, grasp the tip of the needle with pliers and pull the shaved section of the leader butt through the fly-line tip.

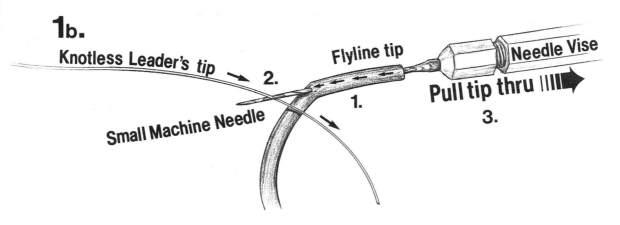

NEEDLE KNOT *(For use with knotless tapered leaders.)*

Step 1B

1. Using a small machine needle held in a needle vise, insert the needle into the center of the end of the fly line far enough that it protrudes through the side of the line one-fourth of an inch from the end.

2. Insert the tip of a knotless leader into the eye of the needle, allowing it to extend at least one-half inch through the eye. Shave the leader tip with a razor blade if it is too large to go through the eye of the needle.

3. Pull the needle back through the fly-line tip, pulling the leader tip with it. Pull all of the leader except six inches of the butt through the line.

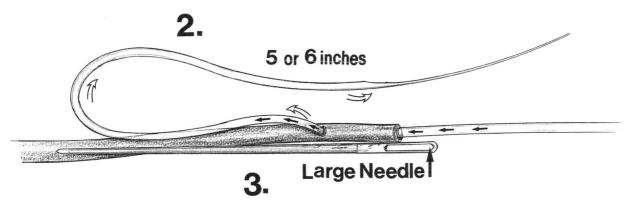

NEEDLE KNOT

Step 2
From this point on the same procedure is used regardless of whether one is using a knotted or knotless leader. Pull five or six inches of the leader butt through the fly line.

Step 3
Lay a large needle immediately beside the fly line with the eye even with the tip of the line.

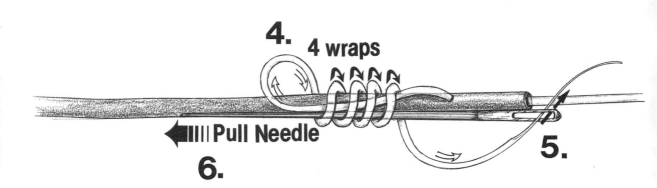

NEEDLE KNOT

Step 4
Holding the fly line firmly against the needle, make four snug, close-spaced wraps of the leader butt around the needle and the line beginning on the needle-tip side and wrapping toward the end of the fly line.

Step 5
Insert the leader into the eye of the needle while carefully holding the wraps in place.

Step 6
Pull the needle, by the point, out from under the four wraps of leader, being careful to keep the shaved portion of the leader in the eye so it slides smoothly under the four wraps.

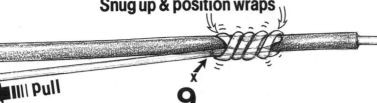

7.
Snug up & position wraps

IIII Pull ◀

7b-8.

9.
x

Pull IIIII ➡

7a-8.

NEEDLE KNOT

Step 7
Carefully snug up and position the leader-butt wraps. I find that snugging these toward each other with opposing thumbnails while holding the fly line in one hand and the leader in the other hand simplifies the job.

Step 7A
Pull the leader to take out the majority of the slack and to begin seating the knot.

Step 7B
Pull the tag end of the leader as you pull on the main part of the leader, being careful to retain the neat wraps around the line.

Step 8
Make a hard pull on both the leader and the tag end to seat and lock the knot properly into place.

Step 9
Trim the excess end of the tag end of the leader butt close to the knot.

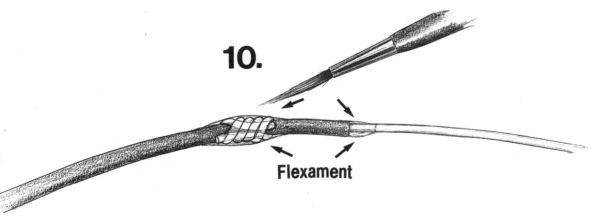

10.

Flexament

NEEDLE KNOT

Step 10
Coat the knot and the tip of the fly line with a flexible waterproof cement such as Flexament or Pliobond.

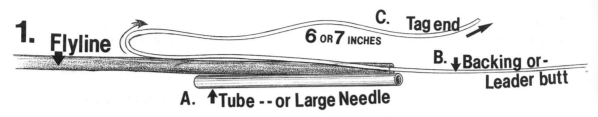

1. Flyline

C. Tag end

6 OR 7 INCHES

B. ↓Backing or-Leader butt

A. ↑Tube -- or Large Needle

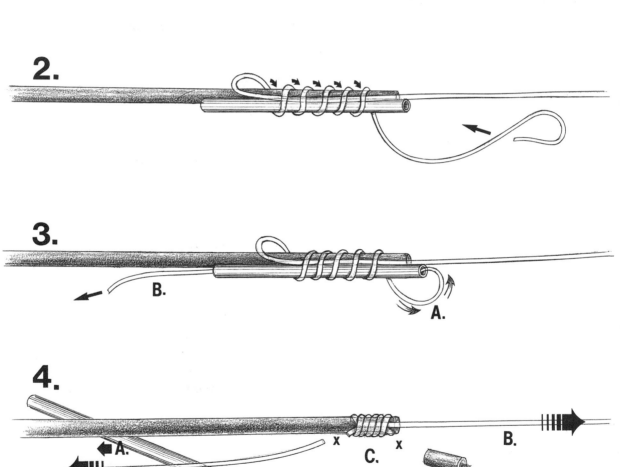

2.

3.

B.

A.

4.

A.

x   **C.**   x

B.

TUBE OR NAIL KNOT *This knot can be used to attach both Dacron backing and the leader to the fly line. The needle knot is preferred for the leader attachment since it makes a much smoother knot.*

Step 1

A. *Lay a two-inch section of a tube (such as a small-diameter soda straw) or a large needle tight along the side of the end of the fly line.*

B. *Lay six or seven inches of the end of the butt of the leader along beside the tube.*

C. *Hold this in place as you fold the tag end forward.*

Step 2

While holding the fly line, the tube, and the leader butt firmly in place make five wraps of the leader butt around the entire unit as the drawing shows.

Step 3

A. *Holding the wraps firmly in place, insert the tag end of the leader in the tube (or the eye of the needle if that is used).*

B. *Slide the leader butt all the way through the tube.*

Step 4

A. *Remove the tube (or the needle) by pulling it in the direction opposite that of the end of the fly line.*

B. *Being careful not to loosen any of the wraps, pull on the main part of the leader and the tag end of the leader to begin drawing down the wraps.*

C. *Snug up and make any final positioning of the wraps necessary so they are uniform and firmly against each other. Now completely seat the knot by pulling firmly on both the leader and the tag end of the leader. Cut off the excessive tag-end tight against the knot and any extra long part of the fly line. (Optional—coat with a flexible cement such as Flexament or Pliobond if desired.)*

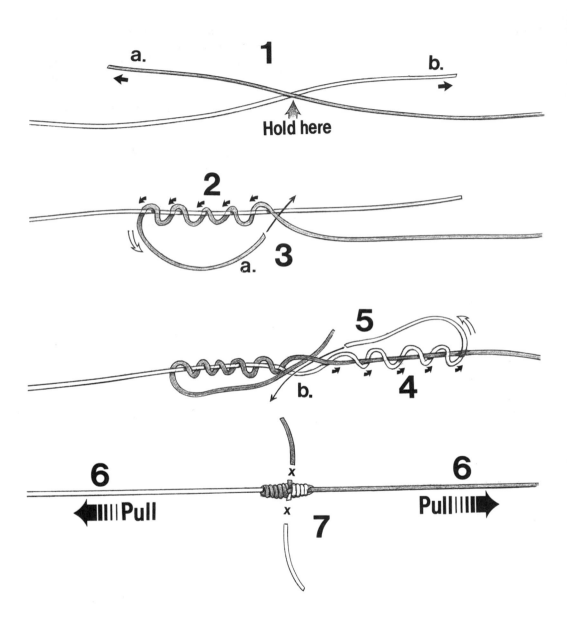

1

a.

b.

Hold here

2

3

a.

5

4

b.

6

6

x

◄║║║Pull

Pull║║║►

x

7

BLOOD KNOT *(Used for building knotted leaders and for replacing tippets.)*

Step 1
Cross the tag ends of the two pieces of leader materials (a and b) to be joined, allowing about three inches of each piece to extend beyond the point of crossing. Hold this point of crossing with your thumb and forefinger.

Step 2
Wrap strand (a) around strand (b) five turns.

Step 3
Insert the tag end of strand (a) back through the point of crossing that you are holding securely.

Step 4
Wrap leader strand (b) five turns around strand (a) being sure to wind in the opposite direction from that which (a) was wound.

Step 5
Insert the tag end of strand (b) through the same gap in the wraps into which strand (a) was inserted, but in the opposite direction.

Step 6
Pull both of the main parts of monofilament to seat the knot securely. If the leader material is in excess of ten-pound test, it is best to seat the knot with a jerk. If it is less than ten-pound test a slow, steady pull usually gives a better knot. Some leader materials provide stronger blood knots if the knot area is lubricated with water, saliva, bug floatant, or line dressing just prior to seating them. It is wise to experiment with your favorite brand to determine the best method of obtaining the strongest knots.

Step 7
Trim the two tag ends close to the knot and it is completed.

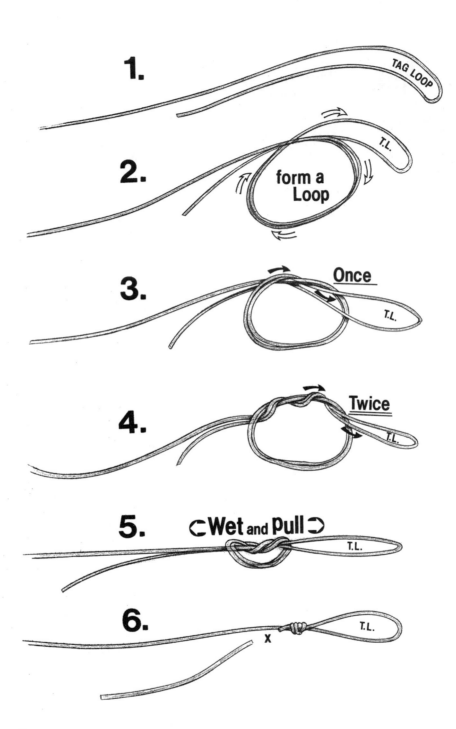

1. TAG LOOP

2. form a Loop T.L.

3. Once T.L.

4. Twice T.L.

5. Wet and Pull T.L.

6. X T.L.

SURGEON'S LOOP KNOT. *(This is an excellent knot to use any time a loop is desired.)*

Step 1
Double the tag end of the leader about three inches, forming a tag loop at the fold.

Step 2
Form a loop about midway into the doubled section.

Step 3
Make a simple overhand knot with the doubled line by inserting the tag loop through the large loop.

Step 4
Insert the tag loop through the large loop the second time as the drawing shows.

Step 5
Hold the tag end and the standing end of the line in one hand and both strands of the loop in the other hand. Tighten the knot by pulling your hands apart. Wetting this knot helps it to seat properly.

Step 6
Cut off the tag end close to the knot.

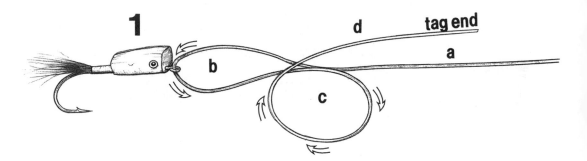

Duncan Loop—or Uni Knot *(This is an excellent knot for attaching bugs and flies tied on ring-eyed hooks to the leader.)*

Step 1
Pass eight inches of the tag end of the leader through the eye of the bug. Allowing a small loop to form at (b) against the hook eye, form a second loop at (c) which is about 1½ inches diameter. Follow the drawing carefully so the closest part of loop (c) is on your side and is the last part formed as you fold tagged end (d).

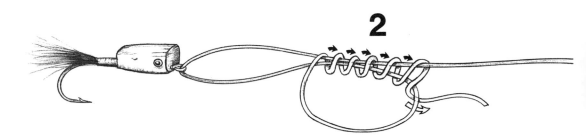

Step 2
Pass the tag end through and around the loop and the tippet five times, wrapping away from the bug.

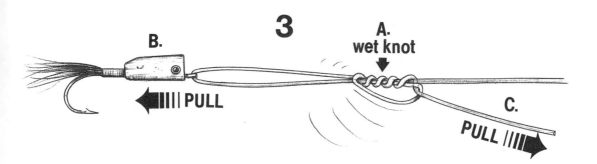

Step 3

A. *Moisten the knot.*

B. *Pull on the bug and snug the five wraps as you hold the tag end.*

C. *Tighten the knot by pulling the tag end. The tighter the knot is pulled the less it will slide.*

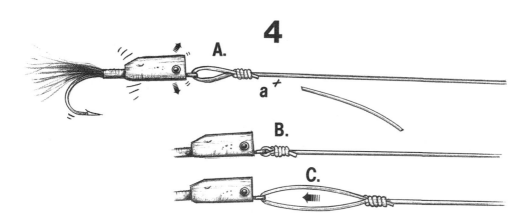

Step 4

A. *Trim the tag end (a) close to the knot. Adjust the loop to the desired size by sliding it along the leader. A small open loop as is shown in drawing (A) permits the fly to have a natural free action unimpeded by the restriction of the leader.*

B. *A closed-down loop, snugged up against the fly, enables the leader to dictate the fly's attitude and action closely.*

C. *A large open loop absorbs the shock of a violent strike or any other excessive strain.*

20

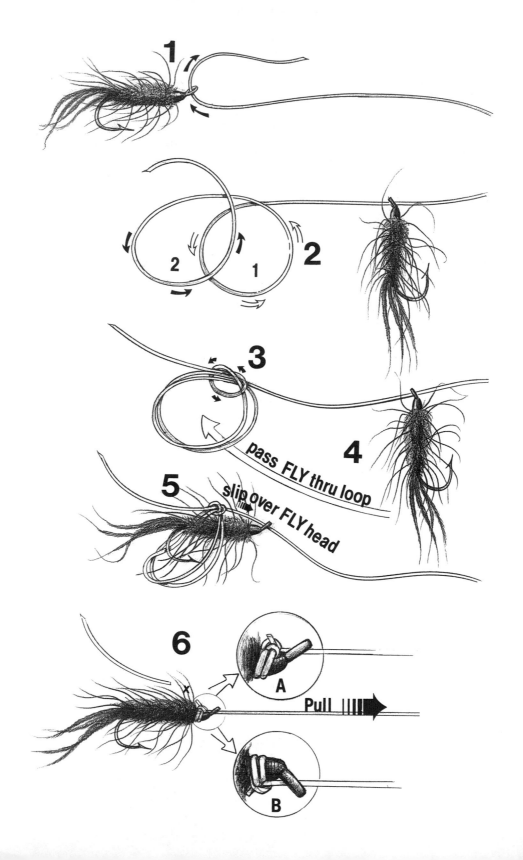

1

2

3

4

pass FLY thru loop

5

slip over FLY head

6

A

Pull

B

SPENCE TURLE KNOT *(For attaching up or down-eyed flies to the leader.)*

Step 1
Pass six inches of the tag end of the leader through the eye of the hook from the side showing the greatest angle. (That is, the bottom of a turned-up eye or the top of a turned-down eye.)

Step 2
Slide the fly about a foot up the leader. Form two loops about one inch in diameter, two inches from the tag end of the leader.

Step 3
Hold the two loops together and form a simple overhand knot with the tag end around both loops. Snug up the wraps slightly.

Step 4
Pass the fly through the loops.

Step 5
Slip the loops forward until they are immediately over the head of the fly but behind the eye. Seat the knot tightly around the head of the fly.

Step 6
Trim the excess tag end of the leader and the knot is completed.
A. This is how the knot should appear on a turned-up-eye fly.

B. This is how the knot should appear on a turned-down-eye fly.

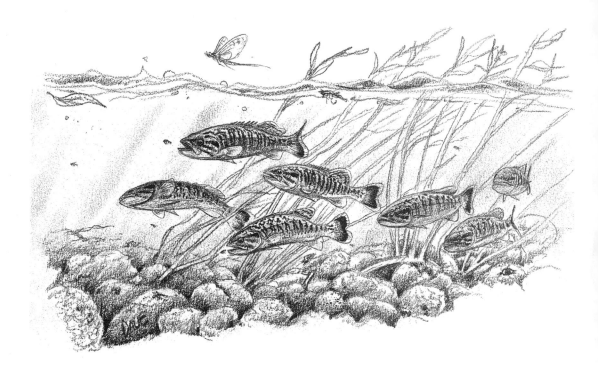

VESTS AND WADERS

A fly-fishing vest is the easiest way to carry flies and assorted gear. If you are into trout fishing as well as smallmouth fishing I would strongly advise having a separate vest for each. The best way to be sure you are going to have what you need on the stream is to put these items in the vest and keep them there.

When purchasing a vest make sure the pockets are large enough to hold the fly boxes you plan to use. If in doubt, take your boxes along to the fly shop and try them out before you purchase your vest.

Try to be sure your vest is large enough, and cut properly, to be comfortable after your get it filled with fly boxes, leaders, extra spools, a rain coat, and maybe even a sandwich. Also consider whether you will be wearing it over bulky clothing in cold weather. A good vest is a great asset but one which is inadequate is an enormous frustration.

There is a broad variety of wading gear from which to choose. Hip boots are inadequate for our purposes—hippers will just succeed in getting you wet. For smallmouth fishing chest-high waders are essential. Chest-high waders come in both the boot-foot style and stocking-foot style. The boot-foot chest-high waders are easier to get on and off, a definite advantage if you want to get to the river quickly after work and squeeze in every second of fishing before it gets dark.

The stocking-foot chest-high waders, with their accompanying wading shoes, are more comfortable than the boot-foot styles. They have an added advantage for the smallmouth angler in warm areas; during the warm months we can eliminate the waders, use just the wading shoes, and wade wet. From this point of view they are more economical than the boot-foot style because we are not wearing out the waders during the summer—just the shoes.

For comfort as well as economy (by eliminating excessive wear) wear heavy wool or neoprene socks between the stocking-foot waders and the wading shoes. Some neoprene socks have built-in cuffs which fit down over the outside of the top of the wading shoes to keep out sand and gravel. Also available are separate zip-up neoprene garters that fit snuggly around the top of the shoes. These are easy to put on and do a good job keeping sand and gravel from getting into the shoes. I use these gravel stoppers both with my waders and in the summer when wading wet.

Use felt sole wading gear to assure a safe and comfortable footing. I like to use the Super Stream Cleats (overshoes with mounted aluminum bars) over my waders in the spring and fall for added traction. In the spring they are a great help in full, fast streams. During the fall, as the water temperatures drop, the microorganisms in the stream settle to the bottom coating every stone with a slippery film. The aluminium cleats simply cut through this film and grip the bottom securely.

Whichever style wader you choose, you will find that a belt worn on the outside of them in the lower chest position makes them safer and much more comfortable.

2

Casting

Techniques for casting smallmouth flies and bugs are not greatly different from those for casting trout flies. In fact, for small streamers and light nymphs there is no difference at all. Heavier smallmouth nymphs require special handling.

The basic maneuver with these nymphs is to keep a tight line from the line hand all the way down to the fly and, with the rod hand, begin a slow, side-arm pick up. As the fly approaches the surface continue with a smooth, up-arching arm lift, utilizing the full arm to get the fly high in the air behind you. At this point begin the forward cast with the full arm in a gradually accelerating motion. The extra weight necessitates presentation almost in slow motion type compared with how we cast a size 14 dry fly on a trout stream.

Large wind-resistant surface bugs present no casting problems if we observe a few simple points. As with all casting it is good to start the bug toward you with the line hand before sliding it off the surface with the rod. One big advantage of this technique in smallmouth angling is that it helps keep the bug on the surface which enables a smoother pick up. A second advantage is that this smooth lift does not totally disrupt the surrounding water—one wants to avoid gurgling a bug across fifteen feet of water surface like a young mallard.

Smallmouth love the shade along stream banks and often a conventional overhead cast will not allow us to cast under the overhanging tree limbs to drop bugs close to the bank. One way to compensate for this is to use a sidearm or almost an underhand cast so the flow of the line and leader on its forward extension is down close to and parallel to the water. This is not difficult to perform if you remember that wherever the rod goes, the line will follow. I use this presentation when I am fishing up to fifteen or twenty feet back under tree limbs that are three or four feet above the water. Sometimes these limbs are down to a foot above,

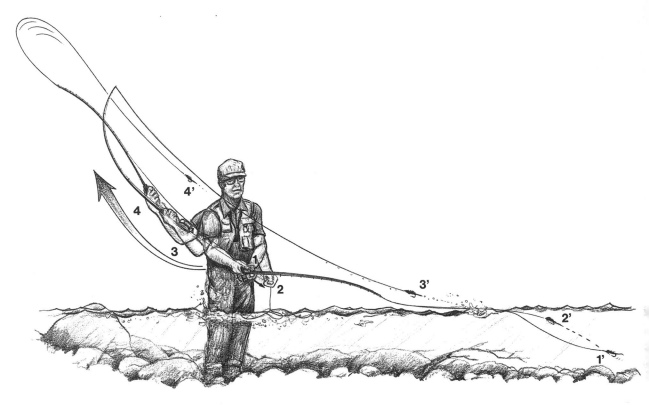

Pick-up and backcast of heavy and deeply sunken bass fly.

1. Start the pick-up of a deeply sunken fly by pointing the rod tip very close to the water's surface at the point where the fly line leaves the water.

2. Use the fly line hand to strip the line over the finger of the rod hand in order to remove any slack line and to start the fly moving toward the surface.

3. As the fly is heading up to the surface, use the rod to begin a slow sidearm pick-up.

4. Continue this smooth up-lifting motion with the full arm until the fly is high in the air behind you. Just as the line straightens behind you, begin the forward cast in a gradually accelerating full-arm motion. This smooth, slow casting style is the most pleasant and efficient I've found with heavy nymphs and streamers.

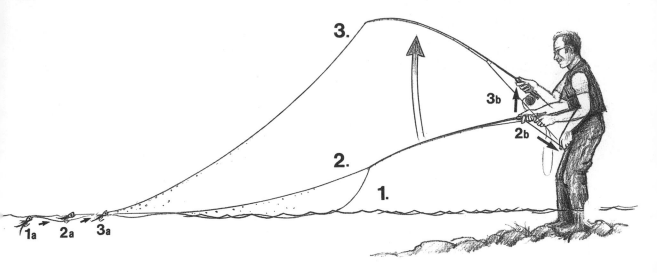

Pick-up of large bass bug.

1. Begin the pick-up of large bass bugs with the rod tip close to the water's surface and pointed where the fly line leaves the water.

2. Use the fly-line hand to remove any slack in the line and leader and to begin moving the bug along the surface.

3. With the bug sliding along the surface, begin a smooth, gradually accelerating pick-up with the forearm while keeping the wrist of the casting arm fairly locked. From this point on the cast is handled in the conventional manner. The two points to remember in picking up large surface bass bugs are to start them moving along the surface with the line hand and to use a firm forearm motion to get them airborne.

or in some cases brushing, the water. These are real hot spots for smallmouth and I'm not about to pass them up.

The best way to get a bug back under this type cover is to get about thirty feet out in the river and about ten to twenty feet upstream of it. From this position you can make a conventional cast to drop your bug tight to the bank just upstream of the limbs. Once the bug and line are on the water I quickly feed slack through the rod tip top by wiggling it back and forth parallel to the stream surface. This extra slack allows the current to pull the bug back under the overhanging tree limbs.

Once the bug has reached the upper end of the hot spot I will bring it to life and fish it all the way out from under the limbs. If I have thirty or forty feet of continuous bank cover like this I may make five or six casts to the upstream open area and simply allow the bug to drift further downstream each time before I start fishing it back to me. There is nothing difficult about this cast; it just takes

Sidearm or underhand cast presentation under overhanging trees or other obstacles.

This cast is performed with the same basic motion as the overhead cast except that the rod travels in a plane approximately parallel to the surface of the water. Only several feet of clearance between the water and the limbs are necessary in order to drop the bug as much as twenty feet back under cover. Extra power can be applied on the forward cast to skip the bug under exceptionally low limbs.

a little patience. I think you will find, however, that your patience will be well rewarded.

In that many of our bugs are bulky, wind can pose a problem. If possible, compensate for this by selecting an area to fish which will put the wind on your line hand shoulder and maybe slightly behind it. If, however, you find yourself where the wind is strong on your rod shoulder you can always turn around and shoot your back cast.

Fortunately we seldom encounter extremely windy conditions and we can usually overcome most problems by keeping the flowing line close to the water surface; this can be accomplished by tightening loops with conventional casting or by casting sidearm.

Remember that whatever cast you select, if your fly or bug is too large for the tippet you are using you are asking for trouble.

Presentation of a surface bug under very low overhead cover along a stream.

1. When overhead limbs are too close to the stream surface to permit presentations with a sidearm cast, the bass can be reached by casting the surface bug to an open area upstream of the fish and allowing the current to take it down to him.

2. As the current pulls the bug downstream, the rod tip is wiggled back and forth so slack line is fed through the guides.

3. The bug is allowed to drift until it reaches the anticipated hot spot, at which point it is brought to life and fished out from under the limbs in the conventional manner. If the desireable water continues beyond the area just covered, the whole process can be repeated and the bug can simply be allowed to drift farther downstream before it is brought to life.

3

The Smallmouth's Diet

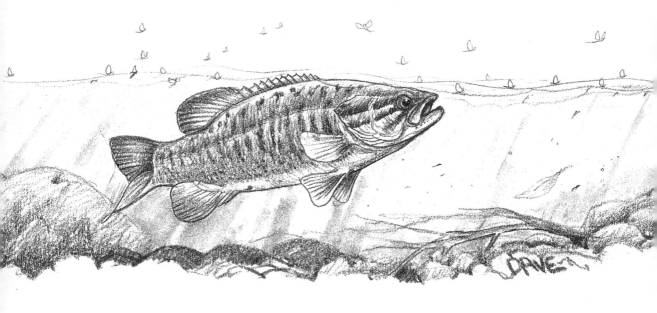

I t is certainly possible to catch smallmouth on flies that represent a food form he has never seen, but an understanding of the natural foods upon which he feeds day in and day out, and imitating them successfully, will improve your chances to take fish consistently. I'm not thinking of those days when you can't seem to do anything wrong and the fish climb all over every pattern you cast; I'm talking about those all-too-frequent days when nothing seems to work. Such days require us to call on all of our knowledge of the smallmouth, and often dig a little deeper, observe a little closer, and analyze a little more thoroughly than we have before to solve the problem at hand.

Frogs

The frog is a favorite food for smallmouth everywhere. Although frogs are excellent swimmers we usually see them around aquatic grassbeds, old logs, and along the banks. Frogs are most active very late in the evening and at night.

The most prominent features of the frog are his strong kicking legs. A well tied hair or cork pattern, with legs that can be made to kick, can be very effective. I get my best results by fishing these "kicker" patterns around the types of cover mentioned above late in the evening.

Mice

Mice provide such a large meal for the smallmouth that once the fish is big enough to handle one I doubt that any poor creature that finds himself swimming past a smallmouth's feeding station ever makes it all the way across. Although mice can swim they have no affinity for the water and in most cases are taken by bass by accidently falling from the banks. Their method of swimming is much like a dog's paddling.

A deer-hair pattern, fished in close to the banks with a slow, steady retrieve, will take many nice bass.

Moths

Late in the evening many moths find their way to the water surface. I have seen large smallmouth come from surprisingly long distances to take moths fluttering on the surface.

Moths come in a broad variety of sizes and colors but I seldom see a thick concentration of any specific kind. I find that a natural deer-hair pattern about an inch and a half long with white bucktail wings will do the job.

Crickets and Grasshoppers

From mid-summer until fall grasshoppers and crickets are large enough to attract sizeable smallmouth. Any portion of the stream which has weed fields or grain fields along the bank can be expected to produce good surface action, especially if there is enough wind to blow a few extra hoppers or crickets to the stream surface. However, even on calm days I have had excellent results by fishing a

size 10 Dave's Hopper tight against these banks; the bass are accustomed to seeing them and take our offerings willingly.

Crickets are productive in the same areas. Dave's Cricket and Ed Shenk's Cricket are both excellent patterns.

Mayflies

Adult mayflies will often bring smallmouth to the surface when things are right. Basically this means either a modest hatch of a fairly large fly, such as a size 8 or 10 Brown Drake, or a very heavy hatch of a smaller fly such as the White Miller. I have seen hundreds of smallmouth simultaneously feeding upon such hatches and it provides some of the most enjoyable fly rodding to be found anywhere.

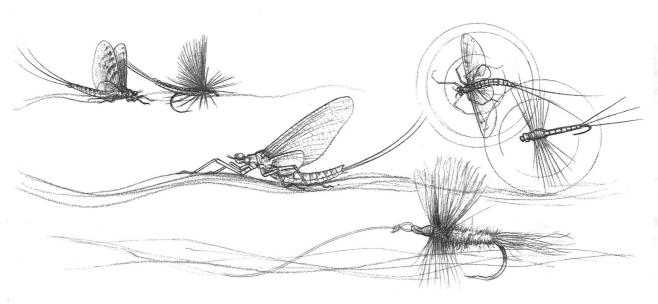

Damselflies

Both the adult and the nymph of this fly attract smallmouth. There is a broad variety of colors in the adults—ranging from black to purple to green to red—and all bring up the fish. The sparse wings and slim bodies of these flies have prompted some anglers to overlook them as a significant smallmouth food, but I have caught bass so stuffed with damselflies that they would be protruding from the fishes' throats.

Grassbeds extending above the water surface, brush piles, and downed tree tops are ideal places to find adult damselflies.

The same areas are good locations for damselfly nymphs. These nymphs are excellent swimmers and their darting action can be well matched with flies.

Dragonflies

The large size of this fly, both in the adult and nymph form, holds much appeal for the smallmouth. This more than offsets the fact that they are not normally as numerous on smallmouth waters as damselflies. I have seen many smallmouth leap into the air in an attempt to capture adult dragonflies buzzing across the stream surface; in fact I have cashed in on this to catch many good bass so located.

Dragonfly nymphs are robust little fellows that swim across the stream bottom with jet-like spurts. An artificial dragonfly nymph, fished over a silty part of the stream with a deliberate darting action, will produce many nice smallmouth bass.

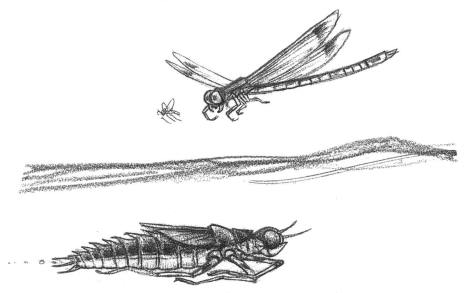

Caddisflies

Thick concentrations of caddisflies on many waters really turn the bass on at certain times of the year. The nymphs of this insect (actually the larva and pupa, but in fly-fisher's lingo, for simplification, we call all of the aquatic forms nymphs) live in rocks and gravel of the fast-water portions of streams.

Sculpin Minnows

As a youngster I sold minnows to the bait fishermen on the Shenandoah River, and the sculpin was always a hot item. Actually most sculpins require better water quality than do smallmouth bass.

I was surprised recently to see the number of sculpins two young boys had seined on a large eastern bass river. Thirty years ago there were no sculpins at all in that part of the river. When the municipal and industrial effluence into this river were cleaned up, the sculpins dropped down into the main river from a small pure-water feeder stream. Now they are one of the primary food items for smallmouth in that river.

These minnows are bottom huggers and prefer to make their homes around and under grapefruit-size rocks in the riffle areas of many smallmouth streams. Well aerated water flowing over such freestone rocks along the banks will also hold sculpins; this is especially true if there are springs or cool pure feeders along that bank. In fact, one local name for this minnow is ''spring minnow.''

I have my best success by fishing sculpin streamers close to the stream bottom just below freestone riffles and along freestone littered banks.

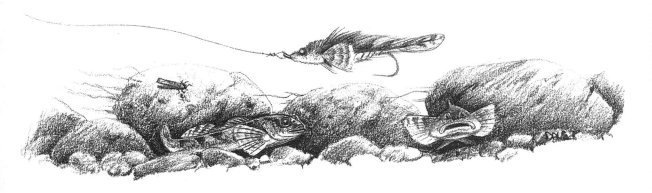

Mad Tom

This minnow looks much like a baby catfish, even down to its whiskers. On smallmouth waters where bait fishing is popular many oldtimers will use no other bait at all when they are after big bass.

Like the sculpins, the mad tom is a bottom hugger. He is most active at night and under low light situations. This does not mean we are restricted to fishing our mad tom patterns in the dark. I often use this fly when I hit the river just at daybreak in the morning, but the smallmouth know the naturals so well that I often use them all day long.

Mad toms are found in the same waters as sculpin but they are also found where the current is slightly slower and the bottom composition consists of smaller rocks. I find many mad toms around baseball-size rocks.

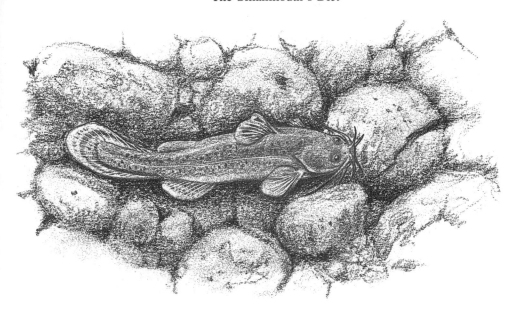

Tadpoles

This juvenile stage of the frog was once the well guarded secret bait of Mr. Will, a local angler acclaimed for his consistent catches of big bass. One day I accidently discovered his secret and was instantly sworn to secrecy. Mr. Will has long since passed on so I suppose it's all right to publicize the effectiveness of the tadpole.

Tadpoles are also bottom dwellers but they live in a different part of the stream than the sculpins and mad toms. I find most tadpoles in water from six inches to two feet deep. It is usually very slow moving water, in fact sometimes dead water without visible current. These areas may be located close to the banks, around islands, and in the shallows close to aquatic grassbeds.

Smallmouth feeding in these areas can be very spooky and it is wise to approach the shallows from out in the main part of the streams; often fishing a long line here will mean the difference between success and failure.

Chubs

Chubs are an important part of the diet for many smallmouth. I find the greatest numbers of these minnows either in riffles or in fairly fast water just below the riffles.

Chubs stay close to the stream bottom but they are more accessible to the bass than are the sculpins and mad toms.

A good chub imitation, such as Shenk's White Streamer, is an excellent searching pattern to use in any broken water since these minnows are found in so many streams and are normally present in large numbers.

It is often necessary to use either a weighted fly, split shot, sinking mini head, or a sinking-tip line to gain the best results with chub imitations early in the season. The bass are accustomed to seeing the real chubs close to the bottom and that's where we want our flies. By mid-summer a floating fly line will usually accomplish this properly in all but the very fastest water.

Shiners

This minnow, and many of his look-alikes with dark back and silvery sides, is found in large numbers throughout the shallow-water areas of many smallmouth waters. It is not at all unusual to see dozens of them dart away as we wade into a stream.

Shiners are fast swimmers but the smallmouth are faster. The bass dart into the shallows or grassbeds to grab a quick meal, then swiftly return to the safety of deeper water close by. I see the most activity in these areas early in the morning and late in the evening and on heavily overcast days when the bass apparently do not feel highly exposed in the shallow water.

Hellgrammites

There are normally more hellgrammites in smallmouth streams than any other large aquatic insect. I have often seen two dozen in one square yard of stream bottom. They prefer well aerated riffles made up of golf-ball to volleyball-size rocks.

This larva of the dobson fly takes three years to mature, so there are always hellgrammites in our streams. At its full size the hellgrammite is about three inches long. Considering its size and heavy populations it is easy to see why this is my favorite food form to match when smallmouth fishing—especially when things get tough and the bass are finicky.

Hellgrammites live under rocks on the stream bottom so every effort should be made to fish flies as close to the bottom as possible. When the situation requires it, the hellgrammite is capable of moving through the current with a forceful, undulating motion; manipulating flies in this manner can often be advantageous.

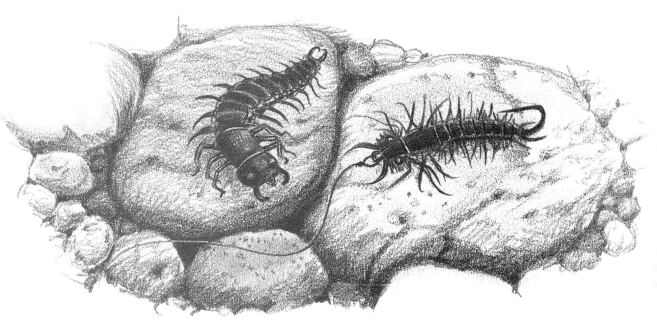

Leeches

Leeches seem to be most active in slightly discolored water and on overcast days, and although I often reach for a dark leech pattern under these situations, I do not hesitate to use them at other times. Most of the leeches I find in smallmouth waters are either black, olive, gray, or brown. They move through the water with a steady undulating body action.

This is an easy action to duplicate with flies, especially with a pattern which is weighted in the forward part of the body with either the bar-bell style lead eyes or chain-type eyes. The retrieve should be slow and steady. If you feel the need to do more than this, as many anglers do, you can apply a slow one- or two-inch stripping action with the line hand, but this is really not necessary. A sinking-tip line and short leader can be a great help in fishing this pattern close to the bottom.

I get some outstanding fishing with leeches late in the summer and in the fall when thick concentrations of aquatic grassbeds are present.

Crawfish

Many biological studies attest to the great number of crawfish smallmouth consume. I find crawfish under rocks from tennis ball-size on up, and in a variety of currents from very fast to hardly moving. I do not find many over sand, silt, or ledge bottoms unless there are a fair number of freestone rocks present.

Crawfish are most active at night and under low light situations, but I certainly would not restrict my fishing with a crawfish fly pattern to these times.

The naturals move across the stream bottom in a slow crawl until the need rises for them to make a fast getaway—such as when being pursued by a bass, when they use their broad muscular tails to swim backwards in a rapid darting motion.

Learn to duplicate both of these motions with flies in both action and appearance. Experience has shown that patterns with exaggerated pincers are not nearly as effective as those with more subdued pincers. The reason for this may be that when a fly is fished deeply the force of the current upon the leader can sometimes cause the crawfish to wobble from side to side in a very unnatural manner. Obviously, the less pronounced the pincers the less apparent this undesirable action will be to the bass.

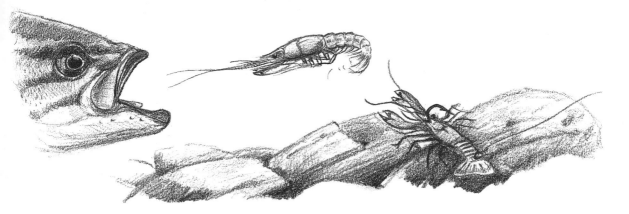

Anglers who would like to learn more about aquatic fish foods or seek a comprehensive study on tying fly patterns to match these natural foods will find a wealth of information in *Dave Whitlock's Guide to Aquatic Trout Foods*. This is by far the best book I have ever seen on this subject and the information Dave presents is equally valuable for both trout and smallmouth angling.

4

Reading a Smallmouth River

Reading the water correctly is the best way to assure consistently good results in smallmouth angling. Without it one is relegated to the old game of "chuck-it-and-chance-it," covering all the water and hoping, by luck, to catch a good bass.

Section of river showing feeding area and casting positions.

Feeding areas

A. shallow riffle

B. deep riffle

C. boulder water

D. back eddy

E. mud flat

F. grassbed

G. gravel bar

H. mid-pool

I. undercut bank

J. downfall

K. cool feeder stream

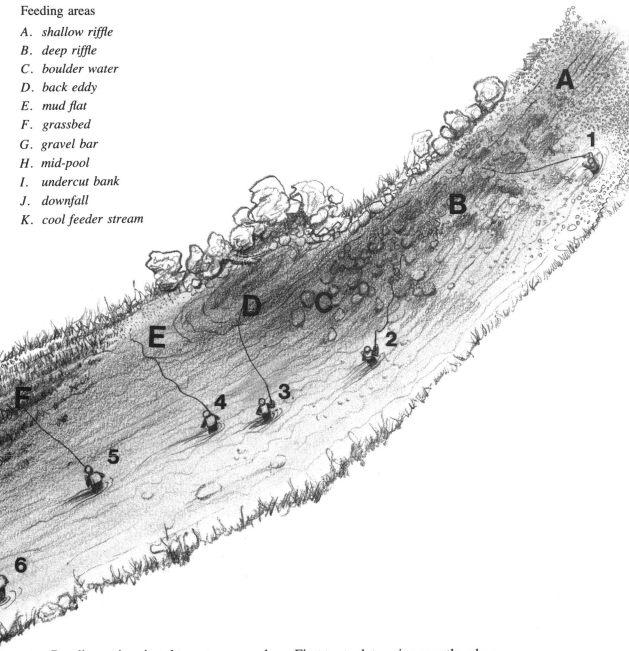

Reading a river is a three-step procedure. First try to determine exactly where a smallmouth will be located. This could be an actual feeding station which he would select strictly for that purpose under specific conditions. It could be a holding or cruising area, located close to a main food source, or it may be a resting area.

Once we feel we know where a smallmouth will, or should, be holding in a specific piece of water we must decide just where to cast the fly. This may mean dropping a nymph ten or twelve feet upstream in order for it to sink to our waiting bass five feet down under a log jam. Or it may mean casting our deer-hair frog just off the upstream edge of a grassbed so we can swim it by the smallmouth holding just inside the grass.

The third step may be even more important than the first two. Where do I position myself in order to make my presentation, and how do I get there? If you botch this part of the game you have had it! This phase takes a little thought and requires a few minutes to evaluate the water, but it is worth the time and effort required. Correctly determining that a smallmouth is feeding on a shallow gravel bar and that a good minnow imitation, darted across the shaded side, should produce a strike is of little value if we approach him closely or with too much commotion.

Likewise, knowing that several good smallmouth often feed on hellgrammites in that deep fast run below a familiar riffle will not help if you don't know where to stand in the run to drop your fly above them so it will sink to their feeding

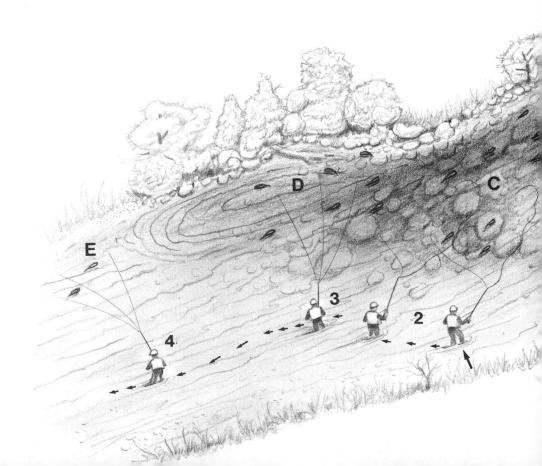

stations; this situation is complicated even further since we must be able to detect the strike in order to set the hook. Your ability to take these fish is going to be determined to a great extent by the selection of your casting position. I have encountered this situation hundreds of times in my fishing schools and often having the angler move as little as five feet will get him into fish he could not connect with before.

In order to gain a better understanding of reading the water let's examine a section of a typical smallmouth river that contains a broad variety of water types. We'll approach the first pool from the upstream side and fish our way down the river.

The riffle entering the pool is typical of many smallmouth streams. The uppermost part of it is made up of a fairly even distribution of grapefruit-size stones from bank to bank. The water here is only about two feet deep in normal mid-season conditions, although about sixty feet downstream we find a number of pockets three feet deep. This is what I call nursery water; it contains many small bass all the time, but larger bass will normally move into the lower portions to feed only early in the morning and late in the evening. (A-1)

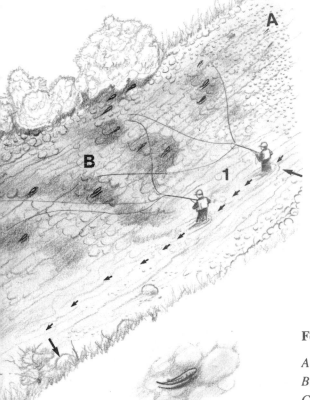

Smallmouth

Feeding areas and casting positions.

A. *shallow riffle*
B. *deep riffle*
C. *boulder water*
D. *back eddy*
E. *mud flat*

Students in one of the author's smallmouth schools spread out to try their skills at reading the water.

This is easy water to fish; the fast current prevents us from scaring the bass and the little ones are not really very spooky anyway. Staying off to one side, and systematically covering the pockets with a streamer using a down-and-across presentation, will take a lot of fish.**(B-1)**

As the riffle drops into the main part of the pool we find a number of boulders which are two to three feet in diameter. The water here is from three to four feet deep. The boulders are not as evenly distributed as the smaller stones were upstream; this, coupled with a few deeper cuts that floodwaters have gouged out over the years, produces a number of different current rates and directions.

This can be both feeding and holding water for sizeable bass. I often think of this type water as presenting a situation for the smallmouth in which the bedroom is located very close to the dining room.

Since the bottom around these boulders is made up of a broad variety of material, from sand behind them to rubble beside them, we find many different natural smallmouth foods. There may be minnows, nymphs, and crawfish here. But there is one thing you can be sure of—they will all be close to the bottom.

If I am wading downstream after fishing the riffle I actually get out to the side of the stream and wade around this water so I can turn and cover it all by fishing upstream. Whether I am fishing a nymph or streamer in the boulder-strewn water I want to fish it upstream, almost dead drift, on a short line. I actually want my fly bouncing along the bottom in every productive looking pocket—behind, in front of, and beside those boulders.

So much of this water holds good fish that the ''reading'' portion of our game is not concerned with where to drift our flies but how to get them there and detect the strike. Hence, our casting position and the target of our cast are of foremost importance. I find that if I try to fish more than thirty feet of line here I do not do justice to the water. It is best to cover the hot spots by intelligent wading rather than shotgun casting. **(C-2)**

Over on the far side of the stream, right against the bank, is a back eddy about thirty feet in diameter. This is now a big, slow-moving back water but it looks more like a forceful whirlpool in the spring, when the river floods and cuts out its soft stream bottom. This one is about five feet deep in the middle so we have to approach it from the river side in order to fish it. The most productive parts of these back eddies are right where they join the main stream flow, and sometimes right against the bank.

Smallmouth don't seem to like the dead water in the middle of these big back eddies, but often, if they are only five to ten feet across, I'll nail a good fish in the middle.

My favorite way to fish back eddies, and I can't seem to pass one up, is to approach them from the main stream side rather than the bank side and cast a streamer right into the closest part of the dead water and slowly swim it out into the current. The strike usually comes right at the slow water–fast water junction.

Since this particular eddy is thirty feet across it will take about six or eight casts to cover it properly. It is important to wade and fish your way around these eddies rather than trying to stay at one spot and cover the whole thing. When I try to cover the downstream portion of one of these eddies from too far above it, the fast water grabs the line and pulls the fly out of the eddy much too fast.

If these back eddies are not over five feet deep you can expect some surface action—especially late in the evening. Remember, this water is moving very slowly and the bass are quite willing to come up and feed on the top. **(D-3)**

Immediately downstream of our back eddy, and adjacent to the bank, is a mud flat. The water is six inches deep right against the bank and gets only about eighteen inches deep as the flat continues ten feet out into the river. This is where we find many tadpoles. The bass will not be here all the time, but it is worth a few casts—especially where the outside edge tapers into the main flow of the river.

The best way to approach this water is from out in the main flow. These fish can be very spooky so easy does it. I like to stay about fifty or sixty feet out from these areas and about ten feet upstream of them. **(E-4)**

As the current picks up, at the downstream part of this mud flat, it brings in more fertile soil and we find an aquatic grassbed along the next one hundred feet of the bank. The grass is thick right against the bank and continues on out into the river for forty feet. The water throughout this area is from one to three feet deep. There are a number of different grasses here but they all fall into the group I call clean grass; that is, the stems and clumps are spaced far enough apart that the smallmouth can, with a little maneuvering, swim back through the grass in search of food. And food this area does hold; minnows, nymphs, and crawfish are all here in great numbers!

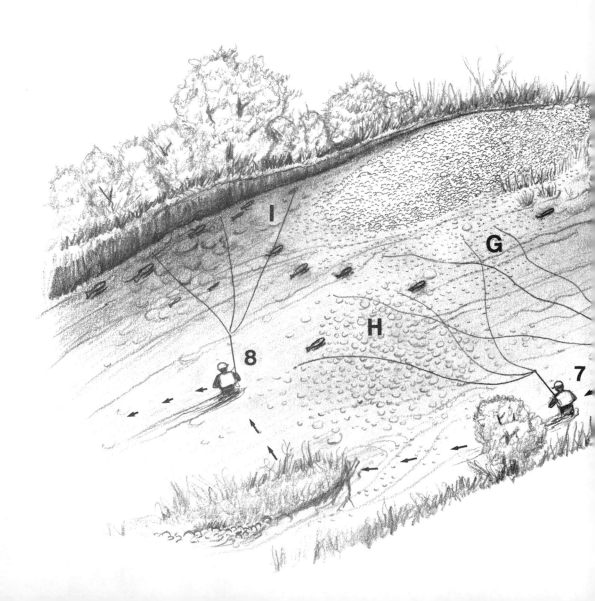

The bass may be found foraging through the grass in search of food, or making speed runs into the edges, or holding just outside waiting for something to stray out into open water. All of these areas are worth fishing. I find that I have my greatest success fishing grassbeds by staying out in the river a comfortable cast away. First I cover the water five to ten feet out from the grass with either a nymph, or streamer, or top water bug. Then I fish the very edge of the grassbed, and last I look inside to drop my bugs into any open pockets that exist.

I realize this may not appear to be a classic case of reading the water since

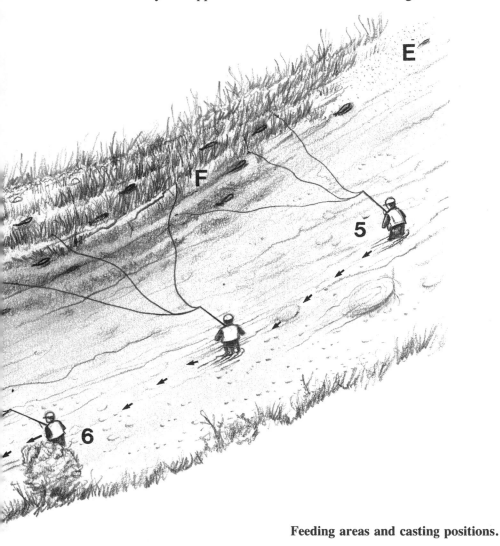

Feeding areas and casting positions.

F. grassbed

G. gravel bar

H. mid-pool

I. undercut bank

we are fishing all areas in and around the grassbeds, but actually bass feed heavily throughout these areas. They may be found in the deeper water close by during the middle part of the day and move more freely into the grass during the morning and evening on most days. But there are enough days when I find them throughout this entire feeding area that I feel I have not done justice to it if I neglect any of it.

Once I catch several bass in a specific portion of these grassbeds I concentrate on similar areas throughout other grassbeds at that time of the day. Often if they are on the edges of one grassbed they will be on the edges of the next one, and if they are far back in the grassbed they will be in a similar area in the next. No doubt the solunar periods, barometric pressures, available light, and hundreds of other factors influence the smallmouth's preference to feed in a certain area at a specific time; but for me an in-depth analysis of these forces takes too much time away from fishing. **(F-5)**

Not far downstream of this grassbed is a gravel bar about seventy feet long. It tapers from a feather-edge back against the bank for about thirty feet out into the river where it is about three feet deep. As with most of these gravel bars this one is the home of thousands of schooling minnows.

Smallmouth feed heavily in these areas in much the same way they do in grassbeds. However, since they are more exposed here they are much more spooky. I fish these gravel beds with a sixty- or seventy-foot cast staying well out in the river from them and often using a twelve-foot leader. Large smallmouth can be much more easily scared in these areas than most anglers realize.

From previous trips I knew where one or two good smallmouth could consistently be found on the edge of one of these gravel bars. On this particular day I approached the hot spot from slightly downstream—wading as cautiously as I could. From about ninety feet out I cast my streamer to the familiar feeding area. The fly line turned over smoothly but while the leader and fly were still about five feet over the water I saw a heavy wake of my bass headed for deep water. The flash of the fly line in the air had scared my fish.

When I discribed this and similar situations to Charley Waterman (who has caught more bass than most anglers have ever seen), I asked if he felt I was correct in assuming it was the line that had scared the smallmouth. After all, why would a large smallmouth bass be afraid of a line in the air which was only ⅛-inch wide? Charley said that he thought the line was to blame. He went on to tell me of similiar situations in which he had seen tarpon in the 100-pound class spooked by a fly line flashing through the air. He said that he assumed they did not see it as an object only ⅛-inch wide but actually perceived it as a flash of light off of something much larger and who knows how high.

This is one reason I often use twelve-foot leaders when fishing shallow areas—especially late in the summer and in the fall. **(G-6)**

The part of the river just off the lower edge of our gravel bar and out in the river about thirty feet is made up of baseball-size stones. The current here is moderate over most of this three- to four-foot deep area. This is ideal water for mad toms.

I fish these areas from the bank side of the runs, casting almost straight across the current. I start at the upper end of these areas and methodically work my way downstream.

Smallmouth feed heavily on mad toms here early in the morning and late in the evening. With the lower light levels and deeper water they will often feed throughout the area for a considerable time so it is wise to cover the whole run very carefully. **(H-7)**

On the far side of the river the bank is about five feet high. There is a moderate current flowing right against it, creating many under-cut pockets back in the bank. The water right against this cut bank ranges from two to four feet deep. This is another one of those bedroom–dining room areas.

Smallmouth can be taken off these cut banks throughout the season almost any time of the day. They may be at their best when they are shaded, but on many streams the thick tree cover along the banks provides this almost all day long.

If the adjoining land is a pasture field which runs right up to the river edge we can expect the best action when the sun is low on that side of the river. For example, one of my favorite cut banks is on the western side of the river. I have never been disappointed when fishing this bank in the evening as the sun starts sinking. On the other hand I seldom do well here when the sun is high in the east. At that time of the morning it is almost like putting a spotlight on the bass. Smallmouth just don't seem to like bright light if they have a choice.

This is one area in which I like to literally "pound the bank." Accuracy here is important. A fly dropped three feet out in the river may not bring a strike but the next cast landing only six inches from the bank may produce the best smallmouth of the season. Some days they will come charging out to nail a fly five feet from the bank, but for every one of those days I've had ten days when they wanted it in tight against the bank. After all, that's where they are holding—amid food, cover, and shade.

Here too the smallmouth sees many land-born creatures. Mice, crickets, grasshoppers, moths, and many other dry land dwellers accidently find their way into the river and are quickly eaten by smallmouth. **(I-8)**

Not far down the bank a large oak tree has fallen out into the river. Part of its root system is holding the trunk tight against the bank but the current has pushed the upper portion slightly downstream. The water flowing under the trunk and through the limbs is about three to four feet deep. This is perfect smallmouth cover.

Most of these down-falls are best fished from the river side since that is the area from which the food comes to the bass. If the water is shallow enough I like to wade to within casting distance out in the river and cover the tree top area with damselflies or shiner-type streamers.

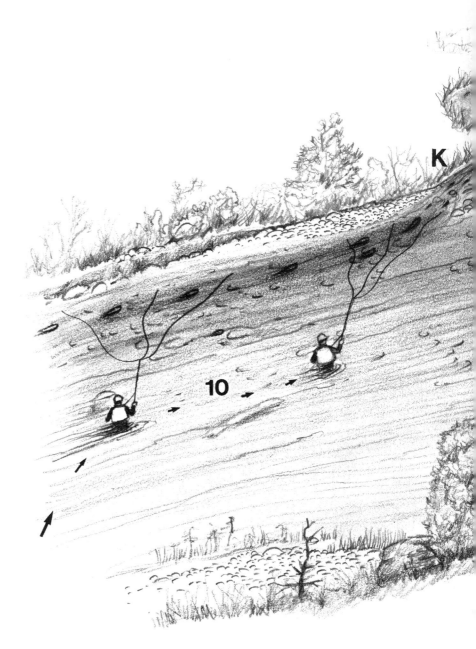

Feeding areas and casting positions.

J. downfall
K. cool feeder stream

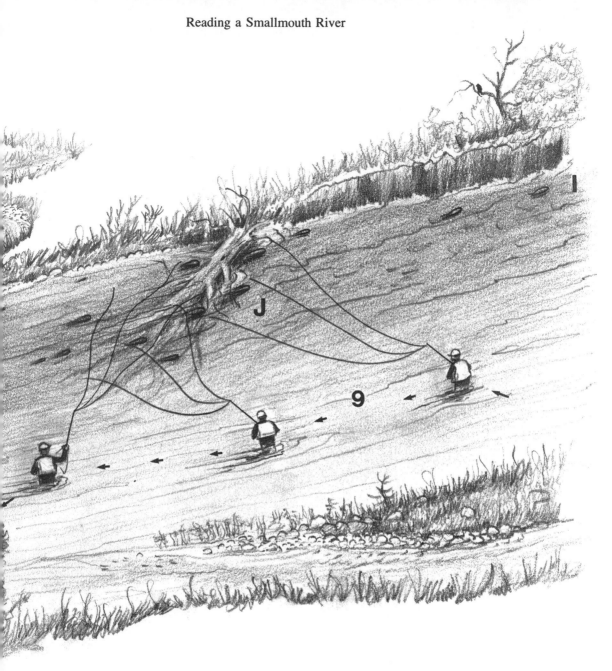

The trunk area will often hold many large bass. Dropping a deer-hair frog against the trunk and gently kicking it away can make some very exciting things happen. If you raise a good fish here but fail to hook him just go back in a few hours, or on the next trip, and he will usually be at the same place. If you land a nice bass here and return him to the stream he will usually be in the same spot the next time you fish there.

This point was driven home to me quite vividly many years ago when I first started tagging smallmouth. I caught a big smallmouth out from under one of these log jams and put tag #23 in his jaw. Several weeks later I fished the same area and sure enough I caught #23 out from under the same log.

On succeeding trips into this general area if the fishing was tough I could always swing over and catch old #23. One of my angling friends later had the audacity to name this fish "Ol Dumb-Dumb." (J-9)

About 200 feet downstream a small cool feeder stream enters our river. This stream is spring fed so it normally assures us of cool pure water, but it flows through cultivated farm land so after a heavy summer thunderstorm it can push in some very discolored "quick water." The diverse features of this and other feeders have saved the day for me more than once.

In mid-summer when many of our smallmouth rivers reach 80 degrees Fahrenheit the smallmouth do not feed as actively as they do in cooler water. These springs stay in the mid-50s even in the hottest weather.

The extent of the cooling effect a spring feeder will have upon the main river depends upon the volume of water that feeder produces. Even a small volume is helpful and will reach out into the river and further downstream than one would expect. Although here we are talking about an actual small stream entering our bass river there are two other sources of cool pure water we should be on the lookout for.

One of these is the true spring which forms right at the river's edge and flows only a foot or two before entering the river. These can be very difficult to spot on the bank. In many, but not all cases, they emerge from gravel or ledge structures below high, sloping banks. Only a small portion of such banks produce springs, however, so don't go out of your way to fish below every high sloping bank you see.

The best indictor of a bank spring is the lush aquatic vegetation that grows in the river right where it enters. This may consist of watercress or several other plants but they are almost always brighter green and thicker than other aquatic weeds.

Another source of cool water for our smallmouth is the underwater spring hole. Rich weed growth can be a giveaway here also but not as vividly as it is for the bank spring. Often I will become aware of these spring holes by feeling the cool water on my legs as I wade.

If you are wading and fishing downstream you may have already missed out on some excellent fishing by the time you wade into a spring hole. If you are wading and fishing upstream and detect cool water on your legs you have a much

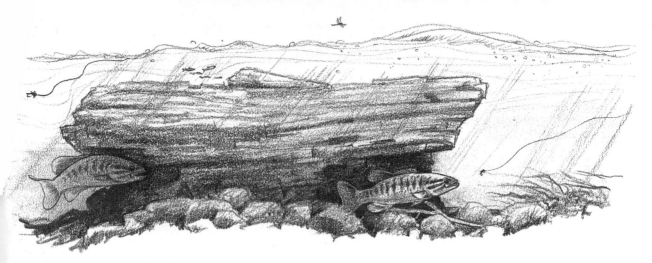

Smallmouth under front and downstream side of ledge.

"Ledges provide excellent cover for bass, but keep in mind that they prefer some slight overhead protection when they can get it."

If you find you can get these smallmouth to take surface bugs you can approach them from almost any angle. However, if you find that you have to go underwater for them the approach is much more demanding.

If the ledges are undercut on the downstream side it is awfully difficult to get a nymph or streamer down deep enough from an upstream angle. It is much better to approach these ledges from downstream and cast your fly almost straight upstream. If the topmost portion of the ledge is several feet under the water you can cast your fly six or eight feet upstream beyond the ledge to let it sink a little more before it gets to the ledge. If, on the other hand, the ledge is only an inch or two under the surface, you must cast your fly right at the downstream edge of the ledge or you will hang your fly on it.

It is difficult to do justice to these ledges undercut on the downstream edge by trying to fish across stream below them. Just as the flies touch the water the force of the current on the line and leader pulls them out of the very spot we want to fish and we must be satified with the small fish we pick up downstream in the less productive water. Straight upstream is the way to fish this type of ledge.

Now let's look at those ledges which have the undercut portion on the upstream side, perpendicular to the flow of the current. Again, if the fish will come to the surface by all means fish them that way. But sometimes we have to go under for them.

You have a choice on how to fish these ledges with underwater flies. You can approach them from below much like we did with the last ledge type but now, since many of these ledges are only several feet thick, you actually wade in right behind the downstream portion of the ledge and cast up or up and across.

better chance of cashing in on the good fishing. Often these underwater spring holes will be coming out from below a ledge or a deep cut and you can just fish your way up to them. I definitely prefer to fish up, or up and across, below a feeder spring creek. I like to start about 200 feet below the feeder and about 100 feet out in the river and fish my way right up to the source.

As I mentioned, this particular feeder stream flows through cultivated farm land and a sudden summer thunderstorm can quickly push in discolored water. This too can be used to our advantage under certain circumstances. For example, several years ago I was guiding a very capable smallmouth fly fisherman in late August. I had taken him to one of the most productive areas of the river but the fishing had been tough. The river was quite low and extremely clear. We simply spooked the big fish before we could get within casting distance of them. I even spotted two huge feeding smallmouth and we literally crawled into casting position, carefully staying downstream of them, and still spooked the bass. Our only success came from fishing across heavy riffles, and that was limited.

Then we got one of those "toad choking thunderstorms," as the old-timers called them. It lasted only about a half an hour so naturally it didn't alter the level nor the color of the main river. But I had a good idea what had happened to the little feeder stream.

We jumped into the car and went upstream about fifteen miles to where the small stream enters the river and sure enough it was very muddy. We waded into the river about 200 yards downstream and on the same side as the feeder. We caught fish like crazy.

The discoloration of the feeder, even though its volume was only a fraction of the river's flow, was enough to prevent the smallmouth from being so spooky. Naturally the "quick water" was pushing some extra food into the river but the discoloration is what really does the job. Just to verify this assumption I fished the part of the river above the feeder, which was just as clear as it had been downstream, and found the fishing every bit as tough as it was down there. Wading back down into the slightly discolored water produced a smallmouth every two or three casts. (K-10)

Back to our typical smallmouth river. The middle part of the main pool runs from three to six feet deep and is about the size of a football field. Some of it is too deep to wade but there are many ledges and shallower areas that enable us to cover almost the entire area.

Ledges provide excellent cover for bass, but keep in mind they prefer some slight overhead protection if they can get it. Ledges are often perfect for this but you should check each area closely to see just where the bass will be located. Ledges seldom have straight sides as they come up from the bottom. In most cases one side or the other will be undercut as much as a foot or two. Realizing that most mid-stream ledges run across the stream flow, this means that either the upstream or downstream edge will provide perfect overhead cover for the bass.

Twenty or thirty-foot casts are best here, to give you maximum control of sinking, fishing, and striking.

If you prefer, you can fish these upstream undercut ledges from above. Not straight upstream, but off at about a 45-degree angle from the ledge and about thirty to forty feet upstream of it.

The idea is to cast your streamer or nymph across stream far enough above the ledge to allow the current to pull it close to the bottom as it approaches the front edge of the ledge. Up to this point you are not actually fishing your fly but should be mending your line and making any corrections necessary in the drift to assure your fly is deep and under control. One caution: too long a cast can result in a snap-the-whip action on the fly when the fast crossing current grabs the fly line and pulls the fly up off the bottom. Naturally, this robs us of the depth we need.

The fly is now drifting along the bottom about ten feet upstream of the ledge. At this point we want to bring it to life and fish it right across in front of the ledge using care not to bring it too far up off of the bottom. If the ledge runs all the way across the river I will often fish my way along its full length by wading a little further out after two or three casts into each undercut.

There is some slow deep water downstream of the ledges. It covers about 200 feet in length and is about 100 feet wide—right in the middle of the river.

Smallmouth in clean grassbed.

"Grass gets thick in late summer and provides excellent cover along the edges for smallmouth. It is loaded with dragonflies, damselflies, shiner-type minnows, and leeches."

The bottom here is a mixture of sand, silt, and fine rubble, conducive to thick weed growth. This grass gets thick in late summer and provides excellent cover along the edge for smallmouth. It is loaded with dragonflies, damselflies, shiner-type minnows, and leeches.

This looks almost like a giant grass island and, although the center is too deep to wade, the upstream fifty to sixty feet and the water coming out from the bank can be negotiated. When the water gets low and the bass get spooky I often use this grass to conceal my approach.

I like to start at the upstream end of this 100-foot-wide grass island and wade down through it about ten to fifteen feet back inside from the edge. From this position it is easy to fish out across the edge into the open water.

Topwater bugs as well as streamers and nymphs work along these edges. Casting across and downstream and playing your flies back up along the edge of the grass will take a lot of nice fish.

I once had an angler in one of my schools who, due to a particular impairment, could not cast a very long line. The water was low and conditions were tough and I realized he was going to scare most of the bass at the range he could cover. After a little experimenting I put him into one of these grass islands and had him wade just inside the edge and fish a short line out into the open water. The grass hid his approach and he caught lots of nice smallmouth.

The extreme downstream portion of the pool is referred to as the tail of the pool. Both banks close in slightly from the sides causing the water to flow a little faster. This particular tail ranges from the one foot deep where the water leaves the pool to three feet deep about eighty feet upstream.

The stream bottom is made up of rocks ranging from four to ten inches in diameter which are uniformly distributed over the whole tail. This type of bottom robs the large bass of good holding water but it makes an excellent feeding area. It is loaded with mad toms, sculpins, shiners, and crawfish.

Early in the morning and late in the evening bass move into these areas to feed. Since this water is fairly shallow with very little broken surface area we must use a cautious approach.

In his wonderful book *Fresh Water Bass,* Ray Bergman describes crawling into casting position in these areas to avoid spooking the smallmouth. Admittedly, this sounds more like a trout tactic than it does a smallmouth maneuver but it is often helpful.

Basically there are two ways to approach this water. You can come up to it through the riffle from below, utilizing the fast water to help conceal your movement. When I use this avenue I actually stay right in the uppermost part of the riffle and cover all of the water I can reach from this spot before moving into the pool itself. If the tail is very wide I will move across the riffle in order to cover any water I cannot reach from my first postion.

After fishing all the water I can cover by casting upstream from the riffle I ease my way up into the pool itself. Slow, gentle wading is a must here. Sending tell-tale waves up into this shallow water will scare all the sizeable bass. Unfortunately this happens without our being aware of it. If the smallmouth just made some noise as they spooked from our approach I'm sure we would be amazed how many we scare. It would probably sound like feeding time at the zoo.

Another way I often approach the tails is from the side of the river about 45 degrees above them. Here I stay back and fish the longest line I can control. I use an unweighted streamer and fish it down and across stream, wading more downstream than across. If, after fishing my way all the way down to the riffle, I feel there is more good water further out I get out on the bank and go back upstream to wade out further and start all over.

This system of reading the water is more time consuming and requires more thought than blind casting. But this approach will definitely take more sizeable smallmouth, and by drawing upon your success here it will help you do a better job on the rest of the river.

5

Topwater Fishing Tactics

DRY FLIES

Smallmouth bass can easily be taken on dry flies. Admittedly certain conditions and fly patterns are more productive than others. By paying attention to existing conditions and presenting the smallmouth with flies which imitate the naturals they are accustomed to seeing, you can take lots of nice bass this way every year.

This is not necessarily the matching-the-hatch game we play with trout, where we go to a size 24 midge pattern on an 8X tippet, but often trout anglers are the most efficient smallmouth dry fly fishermen. I think this is because experience has taught them to observe what nature is doing on the stream.

CADDISFLIES

The first good dry-fly fishing most smallmouth anglers experience each year is when a broad assortment of caddisflies hatch in early May. At this time of the year we occasionally have such high stream conditions that we cannot cash in on this action, but it is wise to keep an eye out for it. The flies will definitely be hatching and if the water level is manageable the action will be fast and furious.

I get my best dry caddisfly fishing from sunset until dark. At this time of the day the adult flies become concentrated over the water as they return to the stream to lay their eggs.

The appearance of the specific fly pattern we use is not extremely demanding. However, it should be durable and constructed in a manner that lets us fish it convincingly. The Elk Hair Caddis and Caddis Buck in sizes 6, 8, and 10 are my favorites. These patterns will withstand a lot more abuse from the bass than some popular trout flies utilizing duck primary feathers and hackle-tip wings. They can also be fished with motion on the water surface.

CADDIS BUCK.

The Caddis Buck dry fly is an excellent pattern to use for smallmouths. It can be fished with a lot of motion, which is a great attribute when there is a thick hatch, and you want your fly to say, "take me."

This aspect of imparting action to the fly really works in our favor on most caddisfly returns. Not only do the naturals act this way, but there are so many flies on the water that if we apply a little extra action to our flies it helps get the bass's attention.

The best way I've found to fish these caddis hatches is to wade downstream, casting across and slightly downstream. Most of the action will be in moderately fast currents, so an exaggerated dancing action is fairly easy to duplicate.

With the rod tip held 45 degrees above the water I lead the fly and use my line hand to apply several two-inch-long strips about once every fifteen seconds. Dressing the line, leader, and fly with silicone cream is a great help in achieving the dancing action. Long casts are not needed here; in fact they will rob you of line control on the water.

I use this technique from the head of the pool as far down into the pool as I can locate rising fish, or until it gets too deep to wade. Then I get out and go on down to the tail of the pool, or below the next riffle, to check for more surface action.

BROWN DRAKE

Late May brings on the Brown Drake mayflies. Technically this is the *Ephemera simulans* but several other large brown mayflies are on many of our waters at the same time and for simplicity many anglers call all of them Brown Drakes.

The duns start emerging about 7:00 PM and shortly thereafter the spinners return to mate and lay their eggs.

This is one of the largest mayflies I see on our stream in large numbers. It is a size 8 and is well matched by an Irresistible, Brown Drake or even an American March Brown tied in that size.

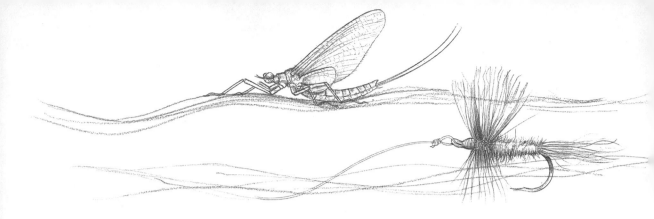

The Brown Drake mayfly is large enough to attract the attention of any respectable smallmouth. Charley Waterman's advice of, "hitting the risers on the head," will take many bass during the heavy spinner falls.

These flies hatch from a broad variety of water types but some of my most memorable days have come from the slow-water portions of the rivers when the spent spinners fall to the stream surface after mating and depositing their eggs.

One evening a friend and I were floating the Shenandoah River in Virginia. We had just finished fishing a riffle, picking up a fair number of fish on streamers, and drifted into a huge flat pool. We could see hundreds of rising smallmouth.

My partner cast his streamer to several of the risers but had no takes. He looked back at where I was seated paddling the canoe to ask what was going on. Rather than go into a lengthy explanation I reached out with the canoe paddle and picked up one of the spent Brown Drake Spinners floating close by and pushed the paddle forward for him to see. He didn't say one word, but I'm sure he came close to a world's speed record for getting a streamer off of the leader and putting on a dry fly.

There are several different ways to fish the Brown Drake for smallmouth. Most anglers talk about the spinners but actually the hatching duns and the returning spinners are often on the water at the same time; the spinners getting thicker toward dark. For smallmouth the same tactics work for both.

If there is a moderate current it is not unusual to find a smallmouth rising in one specific feeding station. This could be just below a boulder, where he would simply stick his nose out into the main flow and pick off the Brown Drakes as the current pushes them to him.

This fish is pretty easy to take. Simply wade into casting position below him and cast your fly about two feet above him on a 3X leader and let the current bring it to him. You should take a good number of fish this way.

Unfortunately not all smallmouth choose this tactic for feeding on Brown Drakes. Some prefer to move around, taking one fly here and one fly there. These fish are called cruisers. They can be tougher to take because other than the one second when they sucked in that last fly you are not sure exactly where they are.

That same evening I just mentioned, when we drifted into the large deep, flat pool in my canoe, all of our fish were cruisers. This is understandable considering that the current in large deep pools is much slower than in the riffles and runs. The current simply does not bring the flies to the bass as fast as they want them, so they go out in search of them.

If there are a fair number of spent flies on the surface one tactic which works well is to anticipate the rise. Watch the rise forms of a feeding bass and try to determine his course. Judge his timing and cast your fly out in front of his anticipated path. Naturally, there is a chance that you have been incorrect in your evaluation of the situation, or that he may swing sharply off course at the last second.

In order to compensate for this I twitch my fly on the surface after letting it lie motionless for fifteen to twenty seconds. Although the natural spinners produce little or no movement this extra action imparted to the artificial often attracts the bass's attention and produces a solid strike.

Another game I play with cruising, surface-feeding bass is a trick Charley Waterman taught me on rainbow trout. We were fishing a high mountain lake in Montana that contained a large population of two-pound rainbows with a fair number of fish running from four to five pounds. As evening approached many mayfly spinners found their way onto the surface of the lake. The big rainbows cruised about sucking the flies from the surface at an indecent rate. Three of us fishing from the west side of the small lake had modest success by watching the riseforms of oncoming trout and casting our flies out in front of them. Then my wife, Bobbie, pointed out that Charley, who was fishing on the far side of the lake, was catching more trout than all three of us. Thinking there may have been more fish on that side I eased my way in that direction on Charley's invitation.

I continued to pick up a few fish as I went but nothing like the number Waterman was picking up. Finally my curiosity got the best of me and I walked on down to where he was to see if he had found a magic fly for this hatch. Surprisingly we were both using the same size and style fly. When I inquired as to how he was getting so many strikes he replied, "I've been hitting them in the head."

He went on to explain that rather than try to anticipate the feeding path of a fish, as soon as one rose to a natural he would quickly cast his fly to the spot of the rise. His justification was that at least for that one split second he knew exactly where the fish was. I used this tactic that day and it worked. I have since used it many times on cruising surface-feeding smallmouth with equal success.

If the flies are thick and the rising fish are showing regularly there is one trick I use to get my fly on target quickly. I hold the fly in the air by gentle false casting until I spot a rise then I quickly shoot it to the fish. Obviously this would be a tiring procedure if one were required to wait long between rises, so use your own judgment.

I find that splatting the fly to the stream surface often brings more strikes than a delicate presentation. I don't know if this gets their attention better, or if they perceive it to be a fluttering natural fly attempting to make a getaway or just what. But it works most of the time.

DAMSELFLIES

By late May or early June there are a fair number of damselflies over our streams. They increase in number as summer progresses and produce good surface action until October. They are present in a broad variety of colors with shades of purple, olive and red predominating.

Some anglers confuse the damselflies with dragonflies, but actually they are quite different in appearance. The damselfly keeps its wings parallel and extending back over the body when at rest. It has a much slimmer body than the dragonfly, and varies from one to two inches long.

Several of the most productive fly patterns for matching the damselflies are the Elk Hair Caddis, Caddis Buck and Whitlock's Spent Damsel in sizes 6, 8 and 10.

Duplicating the exact appearance of the true damselfly is not as important as having a fly pattern that we can fish in a convincing manner. Where and how we fish it is quite significant.

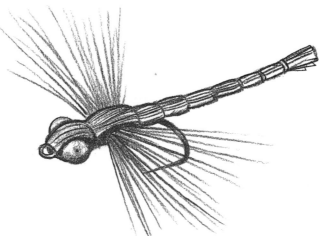

Whitlock's Spent Damsel-Dragon.

Whitlock's Spent Damsel-Dragon will take many good bass when fished close to the aquatic grassbeds where the real insects are found.

One specific day was an eye opener for me regarding the damselflies. I had seen thousands of them on our smallmouth waters all my life but, accepting the old axiom that "they are too skinny to attract sizable smallmouth," I had not fished patterns that imitated them or in areas where I had observed them, even in large numbers.

On this day I was fishing below an old, deteriorating power dam. This was not one of the monsters we see on our large rivers today. It was only about fifteen feet high and, being on a small river, the flow coming over the top of the dam was quite gentle.

I liked to wade in below this dam and fish all the way across the 200 feet of its length, casting my flies right up against the base. Realizing the water was pretty well churned up, I had always fished it with underwater flies.

On this day I saw a fair number of smallmouth flashing surprisingly close to the surface. Finally, after many fruitless casts, I succeeded in hooking one. Upon landing him and removing my fly from his lip I noticed the back of his mouth cavity was covered with adult damselflies; he was so full of them that they were coming out of his throat.

It was only then that I stopped fishing long enough to observe just what was going on. (Sometimes thinking is harder than acting.) There was a fairly strong upstream wind and, for whatever reason, many damselflies had chosen to fly about below the dam. You guessed it; that strong upstream wind was blowing them into the water spilling over the dam. They fell helplessly into the river below, and the smallmouth moved in to take advantage of their newly discovered fast-food restaurant.

I quickly removed the streamer I had been using from my leader and replaced it with a size 8 Light Caddis Buck dry fly. After dressing both the fly and the whole leader with silicone cream I cast it up below the dam. It had no more than touched the water before a good smallmouth sucked it in. I continued to catch bass all the way across the river below the dam. Many of them showed such full stomachs that it seemed improbable that they would really want one more fly to eat.

I realize this was a rather unusual situation but it really woke me up to the possibilities of fishing dry flies when there are good numbers of adult damselflies about the water.

I returned to that and other similar dams later and had more excellent dry damselfly fishing, even when the wind was less severe. But, even more significantly, this experience prompted me to check out other situations for surface action with dry damselflies.

Later that summer I was guiding a fellow on a large smallmouth river. We used my canoe to float down several miles of the river, doing some fishing from it and beaching it in several areas to do our serious fishing by wading. We had experienced pretty good fishing and as the end of the day approached I paddled us leisurely back upstream toward my Jeep.

One slow pool was about twice the size of a football field and most of the water was four to six feet deep. As we entered the tail of the pool we came within casting distance of a brush pile about ten feet in diameter. There were hundreds of damselflies resting upon the brush pile and many were buzzing above the water close by.

I could not see any bass feeding there but suggested my friend cast a dry damselfly pattern in beside the brush pile. He caught a nice smallmouth on his first cast, and went on to take six or eight more from that same area.

There were seven more brush piles scattered throughout that pool. (I later learned that a local resident had put them there to improve the fishing in front of his cabin—he sure knew what he was doing.) We paddled from brush pile to brush pile and my friend was like a kid on Christmas morning. He'd catch a half dozen smallmouth from one area and want to race over to the next one to see if it would produce as well. They all did. Whether such piles are man-made areas of cover or tree tops washed into the river, I always like to check them out for dry damselfly action. They seldom let me down.

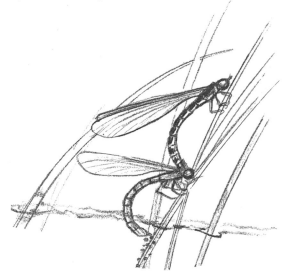

"As the aquatic grassbeds get thick, they become a hot spot for damselfly action. These beds may be as small as a card table or as large as a house, but they all attract damselflies—and bass."

As the aquatic grassbeds get thick they become a hot spot for damselfly action. These beds may be as small as a card table or as large as a house, but they all attract damselflies—and bass. In slow, shallow areas (water six inches to two feet deep) much of this grass will stick out a foot or so above the stream surface. In other areas where there is a moderately fast current through water three to four feet deep the grass will only brush the stream surface. It's tall enough to reach beyond, but the force of the current causes it to reach downstream as it angles up from the stream bottom.

Both of these areas produce good surface action with dry damselfly patterns, but you may want to handle them a little differently.

When fishing the grassbeds extending above the water surface I sometimes choose to come in from downstream and cast straight upstream to them. I like to drop my dry fly as close to the grass as I can get it, and give it only a gentle twitch with the line hand every foot or so as the current pulls it away from the grass. I find that if I fish it away from the grass only eight to ten feet and then pick it up and recast it several feet to either side of the first spot I get my best results. Fishing the fly all the way back doesn't catch as many fish as carefully working it close to the grass.

Another successful way to fish these standing grassbeds with dry damselflies is to approach them from above. Coming down to them about 45 degrees off to one side and using a fairly long line, drop your first cast tight to the uppermost part of the grassbed. Gently fish it out five to ten feet and then pick it up and cast it several feet downstream but still tight to the grass. By wading carefully down the sides of these beds—forty to fifty feet out—and covering the edges with a size 8 Elk Hair Caddis or Caddis Buck you can get lots of action.

Submerged grassbeds, those swinging in a fairly fast run three to four feet deep where just the tops of the plants brush the surface, can also produce well. Recently I took advantage of one of these areas when I had trouble on a favorite stretch.

It was a Sunday afternoon and I should have realized there would be lots of canoes where I wanted to fish. After all, there are three canoe rental companies on that part of the river who put 500 canoes on the water every weekend. Being a popular public river I suppose they have as much right there as we have.

Anyway, the water in my favorite stretch was very low and even when I could find an area out of the canoe's path the fish were very spooky and tough to catch. After an hour with little success—except for a few low back casts which caused concern for several canoeists—I gave up.

Not wanting to quit fishing for the day I decided to try a heavy run I knew some miles above the canoe access point. The area always had thick underwater grassbeds. Maybe getting rid of the canoes and utilizing the thick grass to hide my approach would help. It did. I ended up having one of my best days of the season.

Adult damselflies often rest on the tips of this grass right at the water's edge. It is not at all unusual to see several hundred flies buzzing about over a grassbed the size of a tennis court. There are usually card-table size pockets of open water scattered throughout the aquatic grass and this is where we get our most consistent action.

I like to start at the upstream edge of these grassbeds and wade right down through them, casting my dry fly into all of the open water within range. The smallmouth are accustomed to feeding on the naturals that loose their holds on the tips of the grass so they will often hit flies the instant they touch the water.

The size of the surface opening in the grassbed is not indicative of the size of the smallmouth that is holding below it. In fact, some of the largest bass hold just under the grass beside the small pockets. They appear to like the shade and protection the grass affords.

First-class surface action can be expected where these submerged grassbeds swing in toward the river bank—if they don't quite reach it. All we need is about

Damselfly with bass.

"The smallmouth are accustomed to feeding on the naturals that lose their holds on the tips of the grass so they will often hit flies the instant they touch the water."

two or three feet of open water between the grassbed and the bank. If this open cut has a fairly good current through it and is three to four feet deep you should move some nice smallmouth to a dry damselfly. Both the bank and the grass are providing food and cover and the grass helps conceal our approach. I like to cast my dry damselfly tight to the bank and twitch it gently with my line hand out to the grass and then pick it up and recast it four or five feet farther downstream and repeat the sequence. I'll continue this tactic until I fish all the way through the grassbed.

Fighting bass in aquatic grassbeds can present some problems. We all lose some nice fish here and often it is because we are in too big a hurry. Small fish on strong tippets do not present much of a problem. We simply strong-arm them out knowing that our leader will not break. If it does, few anglers cry over the loss of a small fish or two. However, a big bass is something else.

One tactic used by anglers with calm nerves requires composure but I have seen it work. If a big bass is hooked in open water only ten to fifteen feet from a thick grass jungle these fellows just release all tension on the line as the fish heads for cover. In some cases, the bass, feeling nothing forcing him in a direction he does not want to go, will stop his run short of the grassbed.

One morning I hooked a very large fish on a fairly light leader and, although I knew of this tactic of releasing all line tension, I was not brave enough to try it when my fish headed for the grass and brush. He got into the grass and I tried to muscle him out, only to lose him. I knew that leader wasn't strong enough for that, and if I had it to do all over again I would try the slack line tactic.

The most popular means of getting a hooked bass out of the grass is to move in close and apply as much pressure straight up as you feel your leader will take.

This works in many cases, but if there is much current flowing through the grass it may not. Extra line pressure from above often causes the bass to turn into the current and dive deeper and swim further up into the grass. A tactic I use on trout in spring creeks (often called wet hay fields) has worked well for me on bass also.

Submerged grassbeds in flowing streams seldom stand straight up in the water but angle downstream with the current. This produces many open caverns in all grassbeds. And this is where the bass head.

They may appear to dive straight down, but actually, in most cases, they dive until they find one of these cavern-type openings and turn *upstream* into them—upstream because this is the way the opening is presented to them.

I have my best success in landing these fish by getting below that spot where the fly line enters the grass and keeping the rod tip low (close to the water) and slightly off to one side. If I can achieve it, I like to be able to have the fly line and leader in a straight line from the rod tip up to the bass.

The bass has run into this grass for protection and if we apply excessive pressure when he pauses momentarily it simply makes him dive deeper, and in many cases wrapping the leader and breaking it off. The steady light pressure from a low rod usually does not have this affect.

The bass is down there facing into the current which requires some swimming effort just to hold his own, even if we weren't hooked on him. The low-angled pressure should be just enough to require a little extra work from him in order to stay headed into the current and hold his own. We just want to turn his head slightly. This steady pressure will wear him down to where you can actually, little by little, back him out of the grassbed. Caution, too much pressure while he is still hot will cause him to make a sudden strong run and you'll lose your fish.

DRAGONFLIES

Dragonflies are often mentioned when anglers discuss dry fly fishing for small-mouth. A few of the tactics I use for damselflies will work when the adult

dragonflies are on the water, but the truth is that they are such strong fliers that the bass can seldom capture them. The exceptions are when they first emerge from the nymph stage and really haven't learned to fly well and later when they deposit their eggs.

The Spent Damsel–Dragon fly pattern developed by Dave Whitlock and the old Kol–Ray pattern used by Ray Bergman are two of the best patterns that match this insect.

Skaters

The smallmouth's inefficiency in capturing the flying dragonfly does not discourage him from trying. This ambitious effort prompted me to try something that has produced wonderful fishing on hundreds of occasions.

By late afternoon, one hot summer day, I had fished nymphs, streamers, hair bugs, and hard poppers over one of my favorite smallmouth waters for several hours with very poor results. Seeing a nice bass leap at a flying dragonfly as it buzzed across the surface I shot my popper to him. Nothing! I had just read an excellent story Chauncey Lively had written about Paul Young (the Michigan rod builder) fishing a big dry fly he called the Red Head for smallmouth. I had tied up a few (brown hackle, red floss body and squirrel wings) and this seemed like a good time to try them. I dressed the long-shanked size 6 Red Head dry fly well with silicone floatant and cast it out to the area of the rise. Still nothing.

I was disappointed, but more than this I was curious. Why had that nice smallmouth made such a strong effort to capture the dragonfly buzzing and skipping rapidly across the stream surface and not take my dry fly drifting helplessly on the water? It didn't make any sense, but there must have been something in the natural flies action that said ''come get me—I'm good to eat.''

I remembered a technique I used on trout which Ed Hewett developed on the Neversink River in New York many years ago and decided to try it. Hewett tied a dry fly on a short-shank hook with greatly oversized hackle that he would fish on a tight line with a skating action. The pattern became known as the Neversink Skater.

I had always used the fly on trout with good success, but it had never done well for me on smallmouth. Maybe the short trout-size hooks hadn't shown the bass enough to make it worth their while. But that long shank size 6 I had on my leader may be a little more convincing.

I brought my fly in and dressed that and the whole leader well with silicone cream. Since the skating of dry flies across the water surface is easier to achieve on a down and across stream presentation, I waded several yards upstream and in toward him a little.

I needed only about a forty-foot cast to reach him, which was about right for what I wanted to do. I dropped the big Red Head dry fly about six feet above where I had seen the bass. Instantly I retrieved all the slack line with my line hand and raised the fly rod about 45 degrees over the water. By extending my rod arm as far as I could reach while keeping the line and leader tight all the way to the fly with my line hand, I brought the big dry up on it's toes and skated it across the surface.

Using sort of a stiff arm swing I was able to make the fly bounce and skip along in six- to eight-inch darts. The smallmouth must have approved of this action; it had no more than entered his area before he rose and took it with a splashy, water-throwing exhibition.

Since I had done so poorly all day I decided to experiment with this oversized dry fly in a skating action. For the next mile downstream the river bottom was composed of a series of ledges running across stream perpendicular to the flow of the current. They were several feet thick and ranged from ten to thirty feet apart. Some of the ledges extended above the water's surface but most were from several inches to a foot below the water. The water between the ledges ranged from three to six feet deep.

I used the same technique I had on that first bass. Standing upstream of a ledge I would cast my fly down and across stream to the deep water below it. The instant my fly touched the water I would use my line hand to remove all of the slack line and use the rod to swing the fly to life in a skating action. It worked!

I proceeded to work my way back downstream taking nice smallmouth from some of the same pockets I had fished earlier with a variety of other flies. Wondering if they had all of a sudden started feeding on anything presented to them, I switched back to conventional patterns and had no success—back to my skaters and bang, bang, bang.

Happy with my success, I was a little afraid I had hit on that "one fly that mopped up on one day but never again" situation we have all confronted. (I don't know why, but this does happen.) About a week later I found myself on a different river. My partner and I had covered several miles of water with every fly in our boxes and had taken only a few small bass.

The author dancing a big bass skater dry fly across the surface with an outreached arm and high rod.

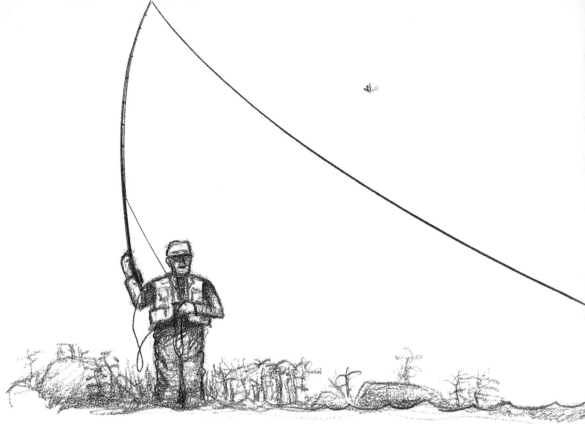

Fishing a skater.

"Using sort of a stiff-arm swing I was able to make the fly bounce and skip along in six to eight-inch darts. The smallmouth must have approved of this action . . . he took it with a splashy, water-throwing exhibition."

Heading back up to the car we came upon a pool with a reputation for producing big fish. We hadn't gotten a strike in it going downstream several hours earlier. The pool was actually a deep, slow pocket about 100 feet wide and fifty feet long in the middle of the river. It looked more like bluegill water than smallmouth cover. Its slow current and six- to eight-foot depth did not look like the ledge set-up which had produced on the skating technique a week earlier, but I decided to try it anyway.

I was very pleasantly surprised when a good smallmouth came charging from the depth of the pool to hit my dry fly as it danced across the surface; I was literally amazed when four of his roommates fell for the same technique.

With this newly found success I decided to experiment for the rest of the season to see just what other types of water would produce with this tactic. As it turned out, the deep cuts between the ledges and the slow flat pools, both of which I had hit upon by luck, were two of the most productive water types for skating dry flies. However, one additional area was as good, and often better than the first two.

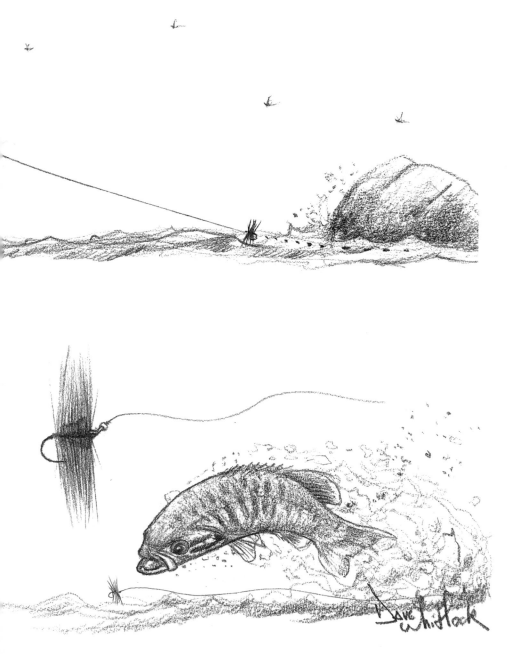

Skater with bass.

"... *a good smallmouth came charging from the depth of the pool to hit my dry fly as it danced across the surface.*"

The long flat tails of the pools were outstanding with skaters. These areas are at their best early in the mornings and late in the evenings, but some produce well at other times. Just how well the pool tails produce during the middle of the day and how far up into the pool you can expect good action with skaters depends upon the physical make up of each specific pool.

The best tails are on those rivers in which the bottom is made up primarily of freestone rocks and gravel rather than solid ledges. This is because a broad assortment of stones—from golf ball to volley ball sizes—provides much more food for the bass than can a solid slab of stone. The irregular sizes of the rocks also provide better cover for the bass.

If the water in the last 100 feet of the tail of the pool contains pockets two to three feet deep around rocks twelve to eighteen inches in diameter you can expect action with skaters here any time of the day. Often this type bottom make up goes with fairly fast water which, up to a point, can help in fishing big drys. It helps hide the approach and simplifies fly action. Obviously, if the water is going so fast that it looks like the lip of Niagara Falls this technique will not work.

In these moderately fast tails with good cover I like to wade downstream and fish them by casting down and across stream with the same sweeping, skating fly action I use over the ledges, except that here I cover all of the water.

If the river is 100 to 200 feet wide I find that I get my best results by breaking it down into several separate parallel runs going downstream. Rather than going down the center of the stream and casting toward both banks I find that if I start by wading close to one bank and carefully skate my flies over the thirty or forty feet closest to me, as I wade downstream, I get more bass in these areas. After I fish all the way to the end of the pool in this narrow section I wade back upstream to where I started and move out about thirty to forty feet across the tail and start down again. I continue this until I cover the full width of the tail of the pool.

If the tail of the pool has few pockets over two feet deep and the current is fairly gentle I seldom do well anytime except early morning and late evening. I pick up a few small bass at other times, but the larger ones are very easily spooked from these shallow tails in the bright conditions of midday.

I even use a slightly different approach if the water looks spooky—even early and late in the day. I approach the slower tails from downstream and cast my flies up and across stream. This makes it a little more difficult to impart a skating action to the flies than with the down-and-across presentation. However, since this upstream approach is used primarily on slower tails, the line handling and fly manipulation are not as difficult as might be imagined. We still want to make the big drys bounce and dance across the surface and by angling our cast more across than upstream this is easier to do. Naturally the higher one can hold the fly rod the better the on-the-water line control you will have. As a result, fly rods from nine to ten feet long are better than shorter rods for fishing skaters.

As I experimented with water types I also experimented with a variety of flies. It seemed highly unlikely that Paul Young's Red Head was the only fly which would work in these conditions. Considering its durability and its long acceptance in many bass bugs, it was only logical that I would try some patterns incorporating clipped deer hair. The Irresistible seemed a logical choice. Although it took some fish in the natural drift, it was a total failure as a skater. It was too dead in the water—the full hair body, even when dressed well with silicone, was too heavy to allow me to get the fly up on its toes and dance it across the surface.

Reflecting on the wonderful success I've had on the large western rivers over the years with the Royal Wulff and Coachman Trude, I decided to try these in large sizes. Both flies took smallmouth when skated across the surface, but the fragile peacock herl bodies did not hold up well to the abuse the bass gave them.

I decided to try some fly patterns which incorporated the fully hackled collar of Paul Young's Red Head with the solidly hackled body of Hewitt's original skaters. Digging through my fly boxes I found two flies which met this requirement. Both were patterns used on western trout streams when the giant stoneflies are hatching: the Improved Sofa Pillow and the Improved Golden Dry Stonefly.

Both flies worked extremely well as bass skaters. They were easier to manipulate than any I had tried, and extremely durable. I used both on a long shank size six hook, which presented the bass with a good mouthful. I have used these for years now and am satisfied with the way they perform in all situations, except

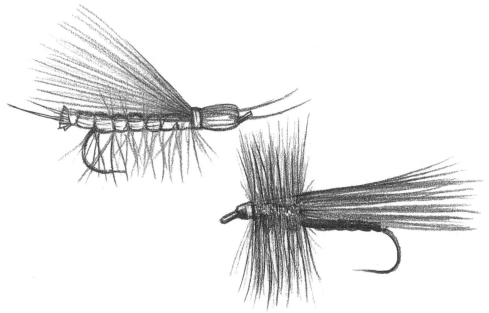

Improved Golden Stone and Improved Sofa Pillow.

Left *(A) Golden Stonefly,* right *(B) Improved Sofa Pillow.*
The big stoneflies ". . . presented the bass with a good mouthful."

one—the shallow tails of pools, where I needed a more streamlined fly to shoot out at the longer ranges required in these spooky flat tails.

Trial and error brought me to the Light Caddis Buck dry fly in size 8. This fly has the fully palmered hackle body of the stoneflies I liked, but the absence of the huge hackled collar enabled it to plane better when casting. I could shoot this easily across the spooky flats even on a number 6 outfit.

As previously mentioned, long rods (nine to ten feet) offer the best control of these big skaters. These rods should balance with 6-, 7-, or 8-weight lines.

Choosing the correct leader is an important part of this skating game. They must turn these big flies over smoothly, and let us be in complete control once the flies are on the water. A stiff nine- or ten-foot leader, tapered no finer than 2X, is about right in most cases. If there is much wind 0X or 1X will work better.

Remember to keep everything high and dry when fishing skaters. It helps to dress the fly, the leader, and the first several feet of fly line liberally with silicone cream.

GRASSHOPPERS AND CRICKETS

By late summer both grasshoppers and crickets are large enough to attract respectable smallmouths. Since both are terrestrial insects we can expect to get our best results close to the banks. I find sections of the rivers which adjoin pasture or hay fields to be the most productive.

One hot summer evening I was walking through one of these pasture fields headed for a good riffle I knew downstream. Not planning to fish the part of the river along the field I walked right along the high bank only several feet back from the water's edge. After walking only several hundred feet I heard some splashing from the river below. At first I didn't pay any attention to it—I wanted to get to my favorite riffle. Finally, after more unexplained commotion tight to the bank, I decided to check it out.

As I had been walking along that high bank I had chased dozens of grasshoppers into the river. The bank was slightly undercut and the smallmouth were holding there, sucking in the hoppers as if they were coming down a conveyer belt.

". . . walking along that high bank I had chased dozens of grasshoppers into the river. . . . the smallmouth were holding there, sucking in hoppers as if they were coming down a conveyer belt."

That was too good to pass up. I walked back upstream along the same path, but this time I intentionally kicked the grass more along the bank as I went. I entered the stream above this undercut bank and eased my way down and out into the river until I was about ten feet above and fifty feet out from the good area. I knotted a size 8 Dave's Hopper on a nine-foot 2X leader and dressed it well with silicone cream. I intentionally splatted it on the water tight against the bank. Hoppers are not known for their delicate landing and I've found that a deliberately hard presentation is often preferred.

Surprisingly, I did not get a strike. Not knowing if I had started a little too far up the river or if I had spooked the fish with a careless approach I decided to fish the cast out anyway. Pointing the rod tip at the line–water entry point, I gave the hopper two firm strips of about three inches each. This made my fly kick across the surface like a real hopper. Wham!

I continued to fish that bank all evening, never making it to the riffle I had set out for.

The bass came well to the hoppers. Some took them as soon as they touched the water, but others seemed to prefer the kicking action. There's no need for an artificially created chum-line of hoppers to find good smallmouth action with this fly. Even a slight breeze blowing across the field toward the stream can push in dozens of hoppers. And even on quiet days enough hoppers land on the water to keep the bass's attention. Naturally the degree of excitement among the fish depends upon the number of natural hoppers present at any one time. This varies from year to year.

I make no distinction between tactics for either hoppers or crickets. I like to cast both to the surface with a little extra force to attract the bass's attention. I usually fish both patterns down and across stream with a kicking action. However, there are times when each seems to do better with the conventional upstream dead-drifting tactics; basically, just casting them in close to the bank and letting them drift along with no action.

In one situation I find the cricket does the best job. Early in the morning, crickets become active before hoppers do, so I usually start with this fly if I'm on appropriate water at daylight.

Dave's Hopper is the best grasshopper pattern I've found for smallmouth. Sizes 6, 8, and 10 will cover most of our needs. Ed Shenk's Cricket and Dave's Cricket are both excellent cricket imitations, sizes 8 and 10 are the most popular.

THE WHITE MILLER

The White Miller (*Ephoron leukon*) is a very special mayfly to many smallmouth anglers. In certain areas this hatch is unbelievably heavy. Smallmouth in these areas probably see more White Millers than they do all the other mayflies combined.

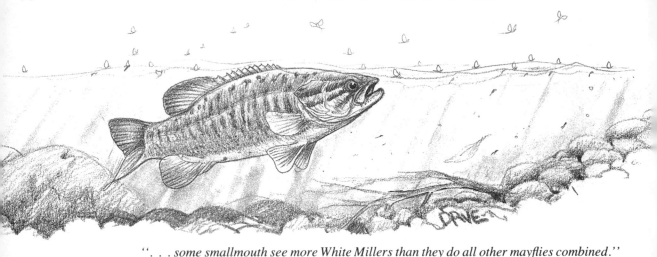

". . . some smallmouth see more White Millers than they do all other mayflies combined."

The flies start showing up in the Mid Atlantic states in mid July. In New York, Michigan, and Wisconsin the hatch lasts well into September. The rule is that the flies are two weeks coming, heavy for two weeks, and two weeks going.

The duns start coming off about an hour before dark. The molting, mating, egg laying, and spinner fall all occur that same evening. In one area I fish there seems to be a fair number of duns and spinners on the water at the same time; on another stream the spinners are so late getting back to the water that fishing them is almost impossible because of the darkness.

The first time I fished this hatch we got to the stream about an hour before the flies started. I did not want to simply wait for the flies so I waded to the far side of the river and fished some grassbeds with poppers.

Bill Burslem and Dick Rabun, who had taken me to the stream, knew the hatch well. They advised keeping an eye out for the duns and changing to a pale white dry fly when they started. The fishing was pretty good right away with poppers, but I kept glancing back across the river in search of the hatch. Finally I saw a few duns, but everytime I glanced back there were not enough of them to bring the bass up.

Absorbed in my popper fishing, I lost track of time. Finally, looking back across the stream, I noticed that a thick evening fog was starting to settle over the river. A second later, as my eyes adjusted, I realized this was no fog but the hatch. I've fished many outstanding hatches on some of the best trout and bass waters in the country, but I've never seen anything like that White Miller hatch. I quickly knotted on a number 12 dry White Miller Dun and had some excellent action.

Some smallmouth select specific feeding stations on this hatch and others move about, just below the surface, taking flies as they go. On a good river with a heavy hatch, there will be so many rising fish that it is difficult to tell which is which.

Bill Burslem shoots a White Miller dry fly to a smallmouth that just rose to take a natural mayfly during the hatch.

A good way to fish this hatch is to shoot your fly a short distance above the rise as soon as you spot it. Upstream, downstream, or across stream—it doesn't matter—just get your fly to him quickly.

Although I'll run a few flies through in a natural dead drift, this isn't necessary and for several reasons I'm not sure it's wise. Let's look at what's really happening. In the first place, the flies are actively kicking and wiggling on the surface in an attempt to become airborne, so the bass are accustomed to seeing their dinner flopping around. In the second place there are so many natural flies out there on the water that the bass won't pay attention to an imitation that just drifts quietly along. Twitching the dry flies, although frowned on in some trout circles, will usually produce many smallmouth strikes on this hatch.

Several different fly patterns are productive on this hatch. Due to the intensity of the action, the short duration of the good fishing period, and the low light level, artificials should incorporate several features. They boil down to a durable, high-floating dry fly with good angler visibility.

Bob Abraham, who fishes this hatch often on the Potomac River, developed an excellent pattern combining a white dubbed body with a complex white deer hair head. I have also done well with both the White Wulff and the Light Goofus, both in size 12.

HARD HEAD BUGS

Hard head bass bugs can be constructed of cork, balsa wood or various plastic heads with assorted feathers and bucktail wings and tails. These surface lures are usually referred to as "poppers." This is somewhat misleading since the popping action is only one of the many actions possible and desirable with hard head bugs.

Ernest H. Peckinpaugh of Chattanooga, Tennessee developed the first cork-bodied surface bugs about 1905. He found that late in the evenings if he could keep his bucktail flies close to the surface he caught many fish. He experimented with putting cork on the hook to keep the bucktail afloat—and poppers were born.

Mr. Peckinpaugh did his initial fishing for bluegills, not realizing their potential for bass until about 1910. Due to a heavy work load he was unable to fish until very late in the evening and at night. Tying these cork bugs on double hooks because of problems keeping the cork on a single hook, he started calling them "Night Bugs." In the 1913 edition of the John I. Hildebrandt Company catalog these poppers are listed as "Night Bugs."

Will H. Dilg, a fisherman and outdoor writer in Chicago, worked with Cal McCarthy, a Chicago fly tyer, to develop various patterns on single hooks. These patterns became known as the Mississippi River Bass Bugs. Several of these hang on the lamp shade on my desk. I'm sure they would be just as productive today as they were fifty years ago, but I'm too sentimental to use them.

Many smallmouth fly fishermen prefer surface bugs to nymphs or streamers. There is absolutely nothing wrong with this. Catch your smallmouth by the method that gives you the greatest amount of pleasure—that's what this game is all about.

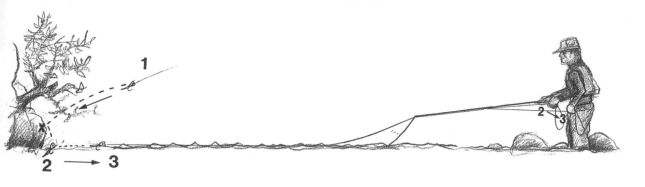

Smallmouth will often respond to different surface-bug actions under various conditions. Experimentation usually reveals the best tactics.

Step 1: *Deliver the bug tight against the cover and let it lie motionless for about thirty seconds.*

Step 2: *If no strike comes in Step 1, I use my line hand to jiggle the bug gently with a minimum of forward movement. I want to make it look like a small animal or big insect wiggling helplessly.*

Step 3: *The bass that resists the first two steps is usually attracted to several slow six-inch strips with the line hand. This produces an easy gurgling, sliding action on the bug. This is a very basic bug action and Step 3 can be repeated three or four times, with fifteen-second pauses in between.*

The trick to being successful with hard head bugs is to match the correct tactics to the specific water being fished. On the first few casts in a given area, I like to use several different types of bug action. For example, if I am fishing a bug tight against a bank, the first thing I do upon delivering the cast is to allow the bug to lie motionless on the surface for about thirty seconds. The bass are accustomed to seeing natural foods fall helplessly onto the surface so a strike will often come before we move the bug.

If this fails to produce a strike I use my line hand to make the bug jiggle gently on the surface with a minimum of forward movement. I want to make it look like a small animal or big insect wiggling helplessly. I'll wiggle it for five or ten seconds and then let it lie motionless for a short period. I'll often repeat this sequence two or three times in an attempt to induce a strike.

If none comes, I use my line hand to make two consecutive, slow six-inch strips. This produces an easy gurgling, sliding action on the bug. I'll repeat this three or four times, with fifteen-second pauses in between. This is a very basic bug action that often produces a strike. When done properly it conveys the impression of a creature that the bass can easily capture.

If, after all of this, I still have not gotten a strike I use my line hand to make two firm three-foot strips in rapid succession. I want to really make a big racket on top by throwing water far and wide.

This type of retrieve—from lying motionless to very noisy—gives the small-mouth plenty to choose from.

When we cast bugs in close to the banks or around grassbeds they often fall onto fairly shallow water. A fast ripping retrieve here would scare the fins off of the bass, whereas a gentle easy action prompts strikes. As we work farther out from the banks the water usually gets gradually deeper. Thus by the time the bug is ten to fifteen feet out from the bank the water may be deep enough that a strong, loud bug action will be required to let them know it's up there.

Notice that I have used my line hand, rather than the fly rod, to give the bug action. There are several good reasons for this. With a little practice one can learn to give many more actions to the bug with the line hand than are possible with the rod only. This is done by stripping the line over the first or second finger of the rod hand. This strip can be anywhere from one inch to three feet and from extremely slow to very fast. Also by using the line hand to give the bug action we free up the rod for the important job of controlling the drift of the fly line on the water. Whether we fish bugs slowly or with a lot of action it is imperative that we remain in control of the action. Retaining this control becomes more difficult as we make longer casts where the line falls across several currents and as the speed of the current increases.

I gain my best control in bug play by pointing the rod tip at the point where the fly line enters the water and two to three feet above the water. From this position it is fairly easy to correct any unwanted dragging action the current produces. For example, if I am casting a bug across and slightly downstream close to a grassbed, as the drawing shows, I want to be able to play the bug in there tight as long as I can. I want to work it gently along ten to twelve feet of the grass as I gradually fish it out. However, the faster current between my casting position and the grassbed is going to grab the line and leader, producing a downstream belly in the line. This will quickly pull my bug away from the grass into the faster water and downstream like snapping a whip.

To prevent this and other unwanted actions we use a procedure called "mending."

Mending is an important part of any fly fishing situation where we are casting across current. The technique is very simple: it requires lifting the rod with a fully extended arm and tossing as much of the line as possible upstream without moving the bug. All we are doing is removing the fly line and leader from the downstream angle and placing it back upstream in line with the bug or slightly above it. An extremely important part of this mending procedure is to use your line hand to pick up the slack you have just thrown in between you and your bug. If the strike comes soon after mending and you have not picked up this slack line you will probably miss the fish. Let's see why.

You are casting to a spot tight against the grass fifty feet away and the current pulls a ten-foot belly downstream in your line; you mend this belly back

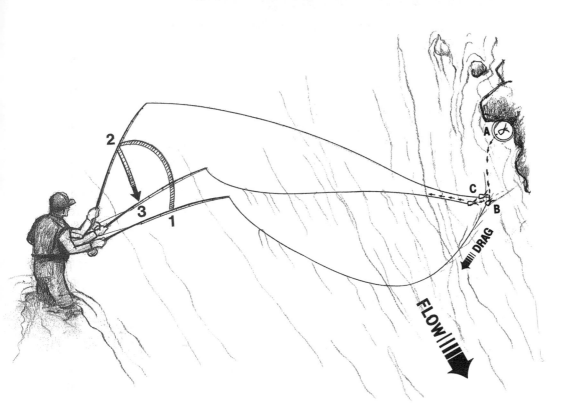

Since shoreline and the edges of grassbeds often hold many bass, it is desireable to play the bugs in these areas as long as possible. Achieving this may call for "mending the line" to prevent a fast current from pulling the bug out from the cover.

Step 1: *As the cast is made the bug falls tight against the bank at Point **A**. The basic slow, stripping action gives the bug the desireable action, letting you fish it to Point **B**. Unfortunately, by this time the fast current, on which the line and leader rest, begins dragging the bug away from the cover.*

Step 2: *Lifting the rod high in the air, with an extended arm, removing the downstream line belly, will permit you to flip the line back upstream holding the bug at Point **C**.*

Step 3: *Dropping the rod back down to a comfortable fishing position, you can now work the bug away from Point **C** in a natural manner.*

upstream. All of a sudden you have more slack line on the water than you can recover when striking the fish no matter how hard you hit him. All you have to do is pick up this extra line with your line hand and you are back in action again. This entire mending and correcting procedure takes about two seconds and it will probably triple the effective fishing drift of your bug.

Another reason it is helpful to keep the rod tip pointed at the spot where the fly line enters the water is to assure better hooking when the strike comes. I have more students miss good smallmouth for this reason than any other.

Fishing across even the slightest current we seldom have a perfectly straight line from us to the bug. We try to minimize this problem by mending, but there is usually a slight downstream or upstream belly in the line.

As an example, let's assume I'm fishing my bug slightly down and across stream to a log jam, as the drawing shows. Although it is sixty feet away, the current between me and the target appears to be fairly uniform. I drop the bug close to the log and, since smallmouth like to lie under or very close to this type of cover, I work it slowly trying to keep it in there tight as long as possible. I'm so sure that I should get a strike here that I keep my eyes glued to the bug. As a result I am unaware that thirty feet out from the log jam the current is a little faster than I had anticipated. This current has pulled a slight downstream belly in my line. Not paying any attention to this belly and concentrating only on my bug, I have my rod pointed straight at the bug.

Sure enough, the strike comes and I miss him completely. Why? Because by having the fly rod pointed at the bug when I struck him I gave him the time he needed to detect my offering as a phony and spit it out. Before the power of my strike could sink the hook in the fish it had to carry all the way around this downstream belly.

The time-delay factor in this sweeping strike is bad enough, but there is another problem—the give of the line in the water. If the downstream belly in the line went from the rod tip straight around a pully lying on the surface of the water and straight back up to the bug, at least we would have a solid pull against the bass when we struck. Unfortunately this is not the case. When we set the hook with that belly on the water, the water cushions the strike, preventing a solid hook up. Simply pointing the rod tip at the point where the line enters the water goes a long way in preventing these problems.

There are seven different styles of hard head bugs, each producing a slightly different action. Nobody carries all these bugs all the time, but an understanding of what you can expect from each style will help you select the appropriate bug for the type water you plan to fish.

CUPPED FACE POPPERS

The Cupped Faced Popper is the most widely used bug we have, primarily because it is the easiest to obtain. Most fly shops in bass country keep a good supply of these, both as finished bugs and in precut bodies for building your own. These poppers can produce a broad variety of actions, depending on how we manipulate them.

These bugs are best for making a lot of racket on the surface. I often find this an advantage when fishing over pockets which are a few feet deep between

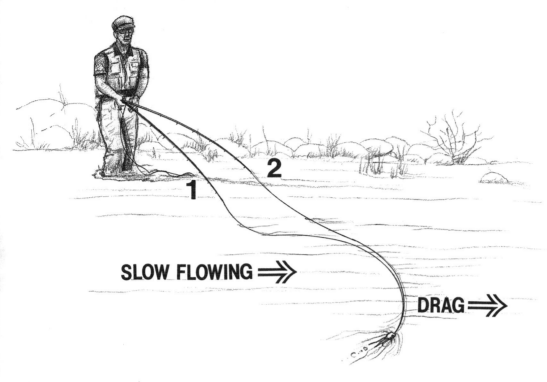

Pointing the rod tip at the spot where the fly line enters the water will increase your percentage of hook-ups more than anything else you can do.

Step 1: When the rod tip is pointed upstream of the spot where the fly line enters the water, an excessively large downstream belly will form, which will cushion your strike when the bass takes your bug—resulting in many missed hook-ups.

Step 2: In order to prevent this, the rod is swung with the drifting line, while the excessive slack is retrieved with the line hand. Now when the bass hits your bug, you can sock it to him.

ledges, if there is a moderately fast current. Staying off to the sides of these pockets and stripping the popper firmly with the line hand enables its scooped-out face to gurgle and pop loudly enough to attract the bass's attention. On some days this noisy action will bring bass up out of these pockets that completely ignored a more subtle action. The same thing is often true of smallmouth in lakes and deep pools in large rivers. It's like the trainer zapping the mule with a two-by-four. First we have to get their attention!

Some anglers, who are strong believers in the great fish-attracting powers of the Cupped Faced Popper, feel that it takes more than its share of large bass. They feel that the extra commotion we can create on the surface with this bug

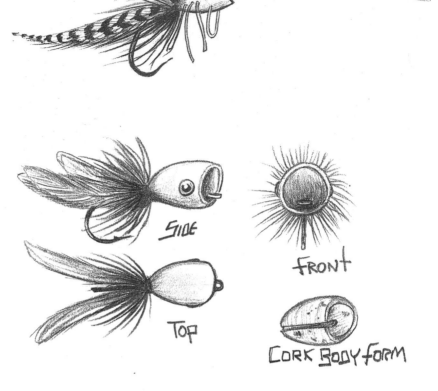

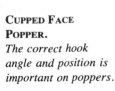

Cupped Face Popper shown from four angles.
Cupped Face Poppers are ideal for beginning tiers to construct. They are easy to make, and the bass will reward you with their enthusiasm.

gives the fish the impression that it is a much larger meal than it really is. There really is something to the ''big fish going for a big fly'' theory. And since we all like to catch big fish occassionally this attribute of the Cup Faced Popper is worth considering. Why throw a bug as large as a humming bird if we don't have to?

Depending on their design, some of these bugs cause beginning anglers a problem by diving under the water when being picked off of the water for the next cast. This produces a loud, whooping noise which could scare the fish and impairs efficient casting. Fortunately a few simple tricks can overcome this problem.

This unwanted racket is produced as we momentarily pull the bug below the surface before getting it airborne on the pick-up cast. To avoid this, use your line hand to get the line tight to the bug as you point the rod tip straight at it. Next start the bug moving slightly with the line hand as you gradually accelerate it with a full arm pick up.

If your favorite Cupped Faced bug is so designed that the pick up persists in being a problem you may try the trick I use occasionally (when I remember it). Dress the leader and first few feet of the line with silicone cream, the same floatant we use on large dry flies and the leader when fishing Skaters. Dressing the leader keeps it on the surface of the water, helping to keep the bug's nose going up rather than under on the pick up.

SLIDERS

A number of hard bugs fall into this category, all characterized by their pointed noses. The most popular one is the Sneaky Pete.

These bugs are capable of several "lazy" actions difficult to achieve with the Cupped Faced Poppers. Their slim, gradually tapering bodies enable us to move them very quietly with a slow or medium-speed retrieve.

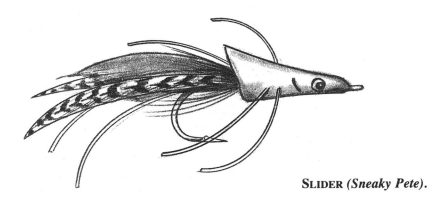

SLIDER (*Sneaky Pete*).

I find this is often an advantage when fishing shallow water adjacent to banks and around islands. There is often a shelf of water about three feet wide against these banks over which the water is only a foot deep. No self respecting large bass is going to stay in such water very long, but many of these shelves have cuts of deeper water close by where the bass can hold in comfort.

I like to cast a Slider onto these shallows and ease it out very gently with a slow, line-hand stripping action—usually the slower the better. The strike normally comes while the bug is in the shallow area just as it approaches the drop off. That slow, tantalizing action is often too much for the bass to resist.

The author fishing a hard-head Slider Bug tight against the grass. A gentle bug action is best here. Photo by Lefty Kreh.

This type of bug play will not cover long sections of a river in a hurry, but we're out here to catch fish—not practice casting. If the fish want a slow action that's what we should give them. It's like the technique one of my grouse-hunting partners uses. He feels we should move through the cover at a fast pace, the theory being that the more country we can cover the more grouse we will get up. Like all theories, it's great as long as it works. Unfortunately there are some days when the grouse just let us walk on by. On these days if we slow down and pause every thirty yards we put a lot more birds in the air.

Water level can also influence what bug action the bass prefer. Most rivers are lower in August and September than earlier in the season. The tails of pools still hold a lot of food and thus attract the smallmouth at feeding time. Late in the season this water is quite shallow and a more delicate bug play usually out performs a more active retrieve.

Bullet Head Bugs

This bug has been around a long time. Companies like Heddon and Hildebrandt and tyers like Herb Howard developed a broad variety of shapes, sizes, and colors with this style of body over fifty years ago. Some of the names were very interesting, but strangely enough most were identified as "minnows" rather than bugs.

BULLET HEAD BUG. *An early name, "Feather Minnow," is a giveaway to the areas and actions to fish with this bug.*

Some of the most popular patterns were the Feather Minnow, the Bucktail Minnow and the Wounded Minnow.

The actions one can produce with these Bullet Head Bugs fall between those possible with Cupped Faced Poppers and the Sliders. They are not as noisy as the former nor as quiet as the latter. But they are capable of taking lots of bass in a broad variety of situations.

The old boys knew their game when they chose the word "minnow" for these patterns. I use this bug with great success when I want the smallmouth to take it for a disabled minnow struggling on the surface.

Starting in mid season many rivers develop thick aquatic weed beds in water about three feet deep. The grass will reach all the way to the stream surface and will be located surprisingly close to some fast currents. I like to work the fast edges of these grassbeds by wading upstream adjacent to the grass and casting my Bullet Head Bug straight upstream close to the grass. I then strip my bug back in foot-long spurts just slightly faster than the current. I try to make it wobble, dive, and wiggle back downstream in much the way a wounded minnow would act.

The strike is normally violent, the bass apparently realizing it must grab the minnow quick before it gets away.

This is an excellent bug to use when you are confronted with a variety of

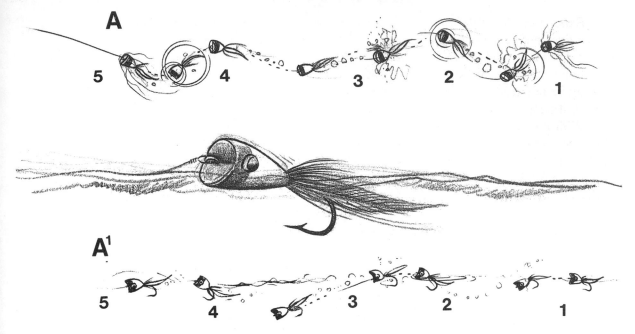

*The Darter Bug is capable of many actions. A good one is the sideways darting action show in **A**, from an overhead view which results, simultaneously, with the diving action shown in **A^1** when viewed from the side. This enticing action results from strip-pause-strip line-hand manipulation.*

water types within a short section of river, and you don't want to use all your fishing time changing bugs. These situations are often encountered in small streams, but dozens of similar set ups occur in large rivers.

DARTERS

The Darter Bugs, with their open-mouth design, are capable of actions which cannot be duplicated with any other hard head bugs. As with the Creek Chub Darter casting plugs of a few years back, they depend on the imagination and skill of the angler to produce at their best.

Simply casting a Darter Bug and retrieving it at a steady pace seldom produces anything except junior-size bass. But altering the pace of the retrieve and making the bug dart and dive about with irregular movements can make lots of exciting things happen.

This is the most productive hard bug I have found for fishing the fast water immediately below riffles. I like to work this water from the side, which allows me to cast straight across the current and strip the bug back in a darting manner.

Experiment—normally a fast, six-inch line-hand stripping action is the most productive, but not always. Remember, we're dropping the bug onto fast water so the instant it touches the surface the current starts pushing it downstream. With this in mind I have often gotten excellent results in these riffles by ripping the bug under, pausing to let the current swing it several feet downstream, then ripping it again, repeating the process all the way across the riffle.

With this technique the strike usually comes during the pause as the Darter bobs back up to the surface. Unfortunately at this point there is a slight slack in the line and it is very easy to miss the bass. To prevent this problem set the hook quickly with both the line hand and the rod at the first indication of a take. Don't worry about taking the bug away from the bass; unless you see him coming it is almost impossible to set the hook too quickly on a smallmouth's surface strike.

The Darter is also one of the best surface bugs to fish over open water four to six feet deep in midstream. The broad variety of wobbling and diving actions possible with the Darter Bug enable us to tempt bass from around deep boulders and ledges.

This is one of the few places where I use a sideways sweeping action with the fly rod to give the bug action. This can be done in several ways, depending on what action we want to impart to the bug. If you are casting down and across stream you can make the Darter wobble slowly just below the surface by using a gentle, swinging motion with the rod to your downstream side. To make it dive deeper and dart sideways more rapidly, swing the rod to your upstream side and strip in a foot of line sharply with your line hand at the same time giving a fast upstream snap of the rod.

To create some unusual actions you can mix these retrieves in order to have your bug jumping every which-way. Be careful—it's easy to become so absorbed with this bug action that one forgets the reason for doing it. We are trying to catch smallmouth, not do drunk duck imitations.

SKIPPING BUGS

Skipping bugs are cleverly designed bugs developed by Bill Gallasch. Their upward sloping faces and smooth lines let us work them rapidly across the surface quite easily when this action is desired. This is a very popular bug in size 2/0 for other species, but for smallmouth size 4 is a much better choice.

The Skipping Bugs produce well in lakes when smallmouth are found slashing into schooling bait fish and minnows close to the surface. They are equally productive when we encounter similar situations in rivers. However, in the latter case timing is a little more critical because the bass are usually after minnows in relatively shallow water. Since they are not comfortable in this shallow water their feeding is a hit-and-run game.

In order to take advantage of this type of feeding it is essential that the bugs

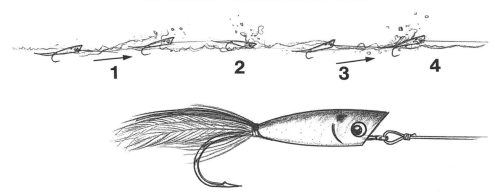

The Skipping Bug is very effective when fished with a varying speed retrieve where bass are found feeding on minnows or baitfish.

look more appealing and easier prey to the bass than the real minnows. This is where the design of the Skipping Bug works in our favor. The game is to cast the bug out in front of the feeding bass, skip it rapidly to get his attention, and then slow the retrieve as he approaches. Make it look good to eat and easy to catch.

PENCIL POPPERS

I have experimented with this design extensively in an attempt to convince the bass that they were getting a shot at a real minnow struggling on the surface. I have tried tying the Pencil Poppers with bodies made of soda straws, hollow wild turkey wing quills, and balsa wood among many other components. I have dyed, sprinkled, bleached and painted them every color imaginable. The bass voted for the balsa wood version in a silver or off-white color.

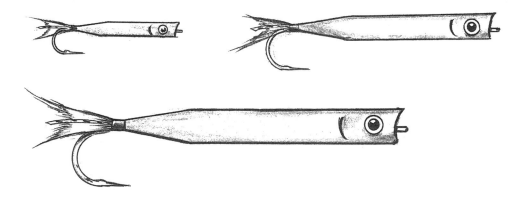

PENCIL POPPERS.
It is easy to fish this bug successfully in many different areas, but the pool-tails, where it can be made to imitate an injured minnow, may be the best.

One of my favorite places to use a Pencil Popper is in the flat tail of a pool. A very effective technique is to approach these tails from downstream and cast the bug straight upstream or up and across stream at a slight angle. Giving a short, pulsating wiggle to the bug, moving it just slightly faster than the current, really makes it look like a struggling wounded minnow. This is easy prey for the bass.

I have also had excellent fishing in these pool tails using this bug another way. In some of these tails there are slightly deeper areas in a twenty to thirty foot section against one bank. The stream will be a little wider here and these side corners will have slower currents than those sweeping out of the center of the pool. These side corners with their slower, deeper water are consistent producers of large bass. I'm not sure whether the bass hold here between periodic forays across the rest of the tail in search of food, or if they simply stay here for much of their feeding. At any rate, when I see one of these areas I give it special attention.

I approach from below, sometimes staying tight to the bank to avoid spooking the bass. Since these hot spots are relatively small (seldom larger than thirty by thirty feet) and the bass may be concentrated in them, I fish the closest area first so the first bass I catch won't scare the others.

In this confined area I don't like to be in any hurry working my bug out. The slower water helps in this. The instant my Pencil Popper lands on the surface I strip in enough line with my line hand so I am tight to the bug, but I don't move it. After leaving it motionless ten to fifteen seconds I give it one slow six-inch strip with my line hand. Pause another ten to fifteen seconds and repeat. This technique is deadly!

Riffles entering the heads of pools also produce well with Pencil Poppers. Casting across these riffles I use what I refer to as a "pop and drift" bug play. The faster current here can work against good surface action, but we use it in our favor with this type of action on the Pencil Popper. As soon as the bug touches the water give it a sharp one-foot strip with the line hand; then pause and let it drift down with the current two or three feet. Repeat this action all the way across a riffle. Use the loud popping action to get the bass's attention in that fast water, then let the Pencil Popper drift helplessly at a pace they can catch.

FLAT FACED POPPER

This is an excellent all around popper in a broad variety of waters. It may not be capable of some of the extreme actions we have discussed but some feel it is the best "compromise" bug available.

Lefty Kreh's Potomac River Popper is the best known bug of this style. Lefty has fished this bug around the world with outstanding results. He is a very knowledgeable angler who has taught me a lot about smallmouth fishing. His

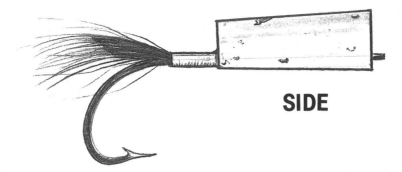

SIDE

FLAT-FACED POPPER.
Lefty Kreh's Potomac River Popper is the best-known Flat-Faced Popper. It is extremely productive in many water types and with a variety of retrieves.

willingness to share his many tricks, tactics, and flies is a welcome contrast to the guarded secrecy of some trout fishing circles.

One great advantage of this style of popper is that it can be picked up smoothly from the surface without diving under. Still it is easy to get a good popping action from it by fishing it with the rod tip at a normal level. I especially like to use this bug when fishing around ledges.

One of my favorite stretches of a nearby river is about 300 yards long with ledges running across the stream every twenty yards or so. Some of these ledges reach above the water's surface while the tops of others may be a foot below it. This makes for a variety of current speeds and directions. What makes the fishing so great is that the water immediately below these narrow ledges ranges from one foot to six feet deep. This assortment of water speeds and depths affords the bass almost any condition they desire on a specific day. The variety of conditions also presents a demanding situation when I want to fish top water here. That's why I often turn to the Flat Faced Popper.

If I find the bass holding in the shallow slow water downstream of a ledge I can work the popper quietly with a slow retrieve. When the bass prefer a pocket six feet deep below a ledge extending above the surface, the slow water does not demand a noisy bug action, but the depth usually means we need more attention getting bug play.

Some days, especially late in the evenings, when the bass want everything to eat that the current can bring them, they will hold at the ends of these ledges. Here the fast current creates a riffle-like situation, resulting from a gap in the ledge where thousands of years of strong currents found a soft spot. The bass seldom hold right in this shoot but move in immediately beside it, still seeking the current-breaking advantage of the ledge just upstream.

This situation often confronts us with bass in water about four feet deep

Lefty Kreh fishing his Potomac River Popper around ledges, where the variety of conditions make this the perfect bug.

with food going by at a pretty fast pace. I get my best results here by casting the bug up and across stream right at the fast water–slow water junction and popping it loudly as I retrieve it right along this edge. Here again, the Flat Faced Popper often does the job.

HAIR BUGS

After all we've said about fishing the surface with dry flies and hard head bugs, why do we need floating hair bugs? Maybe because at heart I'm as much a fly tyer as I am a fly fisherman, and I love to tie them. Maybe just because they are so pretty. But I honestly believe there is more to it than this.

The hair bugs are to the smallmouth bass what the cork bugs are to the largemouth and dry flies to the trout. They just seem to be made for him.

These bugs can be constructed from the body hair of a variety of large animals such as deer, elk, moose, and caribou. These animals grow hair which is hollow, providing insulation from the cold. This same property makes these bass bugs float. Don't confuse body hair with bucktail. A deer, for instance, does not need the insulation in his tail that he needs in his body. The hair in bucktail is more solid and although it works fine in underwater flies, it is a poor floater compared to body hair. Even hair from some parts of the deer's body has better floatation qualities than hair from other parts.

The softness of the floating hair bugs, as compared to the hard head bugs, is one feature many smallmouth anglers like. They argue that once the bass gets the hair bug in his mouth it feels more alive and he is more inclined to hold onto it longer. This extra "munching time" gives us a split second longer to set the hook.

Some anglers also feel that hair bugs can be cast further than the equivalent-size hard head bug.

As with all fly patterns, there are good hair bugs and bad ones. One of the most common faults I find in some bugs is their inability to hook the bass. Not out there at ninety feet, either; some bugs are so poorly designed and tied that you couldn't hold the bass in one hand and the bug in the other and hook the fish. Sometimes the problem is a hook with an inadequate bite (or space) between the point of the hook and the body of the bug, or not clipping the hair close enough to the hook shank along the underside of the bug, or having too many hair legs or feelers sticking down in the way of the hook point.

Some hair bugs are "over-tied," with so many appendages going every which-way that they look like a flying octopus. I'm not sure how the bass feel

The author fishing a hair bug into the shallows along the bank. A streamlined pattern like the Shenandoah Hair Popper is ideal for such long casts.

about these fancy bugs because they cast so poorly that I can seldom make myself use them long enough to give them a fair test. I'm fishing for fun, not frustration.

The most popular sizes for the following hair bugs are sizes 2 through 10.

WHITLOCK'S GERBUBBLE HAIR BUG

This pattern is an exceptionally good example of how modern fly tying techniques can be incorporated with a known fish-attracting pattern of yesteryear. Plus it is one of the most effective bugs I've ever used.

WHITLOCK'S GERBUBBLE HAIR BUG. *"The clever use of lateral hackle wings extending from the sides of the body permits this bug to pass for a much larger food form than it really is."*

The clever use of lateral hackle wings extending from the sides of the body permits this bug to pass for a much larger food form than it really is. This enables us to tempt big bass without resorting to large patterns that are hard to cast. These same hackle wings enable the bug to take on a very lifelike action with the slightest manipulation.

This is a great advantage when fishing the edges of shallow back eddies below riffles. The bass move into these areas for the sole purpose of feeding so we want to make our bug look alive, but we don't want to work it so quickly that we remove it from their dinner table. We can make the Gerbubble Bug just sit there and shimmy the wings with a very slight line-hand jiggle.

Recently an angler in one of my fishing schools started the day off with this bug and caught so many fish on it that by mid afternoon he had everyone else using the same pattern.

WHITLOCK'S MOST HAIR BUG

This series of bugs is one of the best at incorporating rubber legs with a hair body. These wiggly legs really add fish-appeal to a bug.

WHITLOCK'S
MOST-HAIR BUG.
*Charley and Debie
Waterman found
that under certain
conditions "bugs
with rubber legs out-
performed plain ones
by a great margin."*

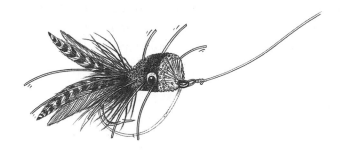

Charley Waterman recently told me of an experiment which he and his wife Debie conducted, using some bugs with rubber legs and some without. Their testing showed without doubt that bugs with rubber legs out performed plain ones by a great margin.

The shaded shallows along the banks are perfect places to use Most Hair Bugs. The delicate delivery we can make with the hair bug and the lively rubber legs are a hard combination to beat here. Slap a heavy bug into some of these shallows, or use one that requires a lot of stripping action to look alive, and you may have already defeated yourself.

SHENANDOAH HAIR POPPER

This hair bug, developed by Rod Yerger, is an excellent all-around bug.

Its streamlining makes it a joy to cast. Even anglers fishing with light trout rods can use this bug safely and comfortably.

SHENANDOAH HAIR
POPPER.
*This bug, developed
by Rod Yerger, is
such a good fish-
hooker that "if you
miss strikes on this
bug it's because you
are napping when you
should be fishing."*

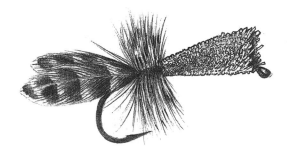

The close-clipped body and the hook used make this one of the best hookers we have. If you miss strikes on this bug it's because you are napping when you should be fishing.

As the name implies, this bug can be fished with a popping action. The late Roy Berry worked with this style of hair bug, coating the bug face with epoxy and other compounds to help the popping action. It really works.

I have experimented extensively with various colors in this bug and seem to get my best results using black bodies and yellow bodies. However, I must admit that the action we give a surface bug is much more significant to our catch than the color.

DRAKE'S SLIDER

The first time I used Everett Drake's Slider I could hardly believe how effective it was. As the years have proved, I wasn't having one of "those days"—you know, like you should have been here last week. It really is a great hair bug.

I've had good success using this slider in mid river in water up to five feet deep with a swimming bug action. Strip it firmly about two feet with the line hand, making it nose under the surface just slightly. Upon pausing it bobs back to the surface; this is when the strike comes. It seems strange to move fish out of water that deep, but apparently that helpless wiggle back to the surface is too much temptation for them.

This is also a great hair bug to swim across stream just below riffles. Its smooth folded hair style of tie lets us fish it like a wounded minnow fighting its way across the current. By mixing the line-hand stripping action with some side rod sweeps you can make this bug do just about anything you want it to do.

DRAKE'S SLIDER.
". . . mixing the line-hand stripping action with some side rod sweeps, you can make this bug do just about anything you want it to do."

DAHLBERG DIVING BUGS

These bugs can be used in much the same ways and places as Drake's Slider. Due to their very clever design and haircut, however, they are capable of more different and more extreme actions than the Sliders.

Dahlberg Diving Bugs can truly be made to dive under very sharply and wobble while they are doing it. With this potential you can see that a swimming, diving, darting, or wobbling action can be produced with the same bug. Although this bug can't replace all other bugs, it sure has opened doors for me. It's the kind of bug that, the more you experiment with it, the more good uses you find for it.

One evening nothing seemed to work for me; none of the normal retrieves with this bug produced any strikes. Out of boredom I cast my Dahlberg Diving

DAHLBERG DIVING BUG.
"One of the largest bass I caught that season came out from under the grass to take" the Dahlberg Diving Bug.

Bug back upstream over water I had just fished very carefully. There was a fast shoot right beside a grassbed and, just to see if I could make the bug dive coming down that fast run, I stripped it very hard several times. It only got about three inches below the surface, but that was enough. One of the largest bass I caught that season came out from under the grass to take it.

Getting more serious about this unusual retrieve I fished back up through the water I had just covered and continued to take good fish all evening.

DEER HAIR MOUSE

The Deer Hair Mouse has been a standard for smallmouth anglers for a long time and still produces well. Since mice are land lovers and not known for distance swimming, it is only logical that we would get our best fishing with them close to the banks and shore.

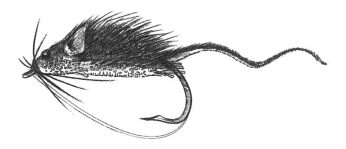

DEER HAIR MOUSE.
"I get my best results by working the Deer Hair Mouse in close to the bank with a line-hand twisting retrieve."

I get my best results by working the Deer Hair Mouse in close to the bank with a line-hand twisting retrieve. I seldom fish it out more than ten feet from the bank before picking it up to recast back tight to the bank about five feet above or below the first spot.

I once fished a nice smallmouth lake near Sudbury, Ontario where one of the local lumberjacks told me of his mouse tactics for smallmouth. The procedure was to tie a hook onto the back of a live mouse who was then set on a chip of wood about six inches square. The chip was set adrift in the lake where the wind could take it out. The woodsman would then freely feed out about 100 feet of line. When the line came tight the mouse was jerked from the chip and made to swim for it. It sounds crude but he said he caught a lot of bass this way. This same guide told me he had one lake on which the smallmouth fishing was so good that he could guarantee a bass-on-every-cast or no pay. Unfortunately the whole time I stayed at his camp he insisted the road was too muddy to reach this magic lake. I never did see the mouse trick or the lake, so they both could have been tall tales among the timber for all I know.

DEER HAIR FROGS

This is one pattern on which hair tying is carried to a fine art. Tyers like Tom Mann, Jimmy Nix, Clyde Houston, and Dave Whitlock tie such beautiful frogs that few anglers want to fish with them, choosing rather to display them on their rod cabinets or hat bands.

DEER HAIR FROGS. *The Krazy Kicker Frog (a modern Messinger style) on the left and the Near-Nuff Frog on the right will bring a lot of bass out from under the grass.*

Deer Hair Frogs do catch a lot of smallmouth and although it is a tough pattern to tie in the kicker style it is well worth seeking out some to carry at all times. I have finally found one person to tie the old Messinger Kicker Frog for me (we call it the Krazy Kicker Frog), and the style is as good today as it was fifty years ago. Dave Whitlock has one pattern he calls the Near Nuff Frog which, although not tied in the kicker style, is an excellent bug.

Since frogs are found around grassbeds and thick cover you may want to choose a weedless version. The most popular weedless design has fairly stiff monofilament wrapped from around the bend of the hook up across the point to the eye of the hook. Properly done, with the right mono, it does retard weed hang ups and still hooks the fish well. But be careful: I've seen some weed guards tied with such stiff mono so far down on the hook bend that hooking the bass becomes almost impossible.

When fishing hair frogs many anglers get their best results by dropping the bug in such a position that they can retrieve it toward the grassbeds or cover as opposed to working it away from the cover. This makes a lot of sense and if you can maneuver your craft or wade into position to achieve it, give it a try. If you have to cast toward the cover and work your frog toward the open water, then cast away. Smallmouth love them any way they can get them.

SHENANDOAH FLYING HAIR MOTH

Deer hair moths have been around a long time but most have been tied with wings sticking out to the sides in what we refer to as a ''spent wing'' style in trout flies. This design is great for trout flies but when used on large size bass hair bugs it produces a pattern which is difficult to cast and often twists the leader.

SHENANDOAH FLYING HAIR MOTH. *''As darkness approaches bass are more comfortable in the shallows close to the bank, and I have often seen them go surprising distances . . . to take a moth.''*

This specific moth bug, designed by Rod Yerger, is one of the smoothest casting and most productive bugs we have. Rod uses an upright wing sweeping back over the body in a Trude style which not only casts well, but provides better visibility on the water. Since moths are thickest on the water late in the evenings this extra visibility is a great help.

As darkness approaches bass are more comfortable in the shallows close to the bank, and I have often seen them go surprising distances out of such cover to take moths fluttering on the surface. When you spot the wake of a bass moving in these shallows get your bug out in front of him as quickly as you can; if your timing and accuracy are good you won't need very active bug action to get his attention.

I often use this bug to just "fish the water" at the end of the day. In this case, not knowing how far the bass may be from my bug, I give it a fair amount of action by imparting a short stripping action with my line hand. This action should be varied in speed and duration to offer the maximum appeal.

This style of moth is also an excellent cicada imitation. Some bass could live their entire lives without seeing one of these insects, but when they do occur some exciting things can happen. Their thick concentrations and large sizes may produce the fastest smallmouth action you will ever see.

TAPPLY'S BASS BUG

H. G. Tapply, of "Tap's Tips" fame and author of several excellent books on angling, created this bug to meet a variety of needs.

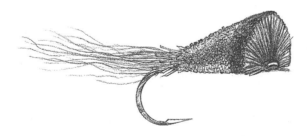

TAPPLY'S BASS BUG. *This bug is easy to tie, easy to cast, and the smallmouths really go for it—a hard combination to beat.*

When tied with very tightly packed deer hair and an epoxy coated face, as developed by Roy Berry, it can be made to "pop" quite loudly on the surface. It can also be tied with a long, slim tail which casts beautifully, yet gives the bass an impression of a whole meal.

Tap's Bug is one of the easiest bugs to tie and for the past fifteen years I have used this as the main hair pattern for my beginner fly-tying classes. Most tyers, with the proper instructions, learn to do an outstanding job on this bug on their first attempt. Not only does it come out looking like a pretty bug but, as they happily find out their first time on the stream, it catches fish.

6

Smallmouth Streamers

The term streamer is generally applied to all flies used to imitate minnows or bait fish. Until recently we made a distinction between the terms streamer and bucktail since the former was tied with feathers and the latter was tied with hair—even though both were imitating the same foods. Today we tie these patterns with feathers, hair, fur, leather, and assorted synthetics and call them all streamers.

The approach I will take in this chapter might be considered a technique of ''matching minnows.'' I will cover various fly patterns which *look like* some of the specific minnows we need to imitate, but more importantly the flies must *fish like* the minnows we are duplicating. By this I mean they must be constructed in a fashion, and of materials, that enable us to make them behave like the specific minnows the smallmouth are accustomed to seeing.

This will be carried one step further in selecting flies that are adapted to the individual areas where specific minnows are found. For example, a streamer worked slowly along the bottom in deep water has different requirements from one retrieved rapidly in shallow water.

Superficially these requirements may not seem as demanding as those encountered when trout fishing on spring creeks, where one might change from a size 22 to a size 24 Olive No Hackle on a beatis hatch. However, taking sizeable smallmouth consistently under a variety of conditions requires all the know-how and experience one can draw upon. Subtle differences of fly and technique can make a world of difference.

BOTTOM BOUNCING STREAMERS

The sculpin minnow is one of the most broadly distributed minnows in smallmouth streams. They make their homes on the stream bottom under rocks which range from baseball to volleyball size. Sculpins like well oxygenated water, and we

104

normally find many more in the riffles than elsewhere. An exception might be where a cool pure feeder stream enters a smallmouth river. Immediately below one of these small streams can be a hot spot for sculpins.

My three favorite sculpin streamers are Whitlock's Sculpin, Shenk's Black Sculpin, and the Spuddler in sizes 2 to 8. All three fulfill the requirements of looking and fishing like the real minnows. This latter attribute becomes quite demanding with Sculpins since it is often necessary to work them very slowly.

When fishing the riffles with Sculpin streamers we should make every attempt to keep the flies as close as possible to the stream bottom. The basic technique here calls for casting across the riffle and mending the line in order for the streamers to reach the bottom, then fish them back across the riffle.

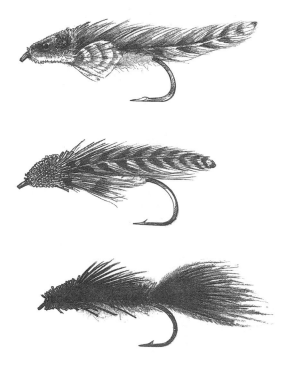

Three Sculpin flies.
WHITLOCK'S SCULPIN
SPUDDLER
SHENK'S SCULPIN
These streamers not only look like the real sculpin minnows, but they can be made to act like them in the stream.

A slow line-hand stripping action where we dart our streamer three inches or so every five seconds is about right. The current is playing the fly all the time, so it really requires very little action from us to look alive (another aspect of what I mean by selecting the appropriate flies). Also the more we strip the fly under this situation the more we pull it up off of the stream bottom—remember, sculpins are bottom huggers and that's where we should keep our streamers.

Sculpins are seldom found where the stream bottom is composed of solid ledges. However, there is one outstanding exception worthy of note. This occurs when a ledge running across the stream causes a miniature waterfall a foot or so high. During periods of extremely big water this ledge acts like a snow fence,

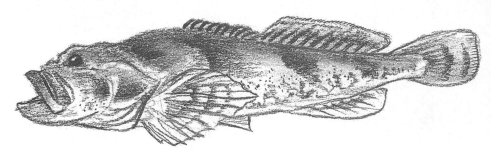

SCULPIN MINNOW.
*Sculpins live under
stones on the stream
bottom and provide an
important part of the
smallmouth's diet in
many streams.*

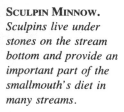

enabling many stones to be dropped immediately downstream of it. We still have a solid ledge stream bottom but now it is covered with rocks and rubble up to grapefruit size. Many of these stone-littered areas may reach downstream fifty feet beyond the snow fence ledge.

We now have a perfect set up for sculpins. The stones provide the homes, and the fast water and rubble provide the food.

These areas are easy to fish and usually produce very well. An effective way to cover them is to stay upstream immediately above the ledge and cast across and downstream dropping the fly just below it. The same slow stripping action does the job.

I will often work one of these areas all the way across a river and then walk downstream until I find another and fish back across the stream. If the river is 300 feet wide it will take over an hour to fish one of these areas properly. And it is not unusual for it to yield several dozen smallmouth.

One aspect of this specific type fishing which many anglers like is that it can be done with delicate rods throwing light lines. On a recent trip my fishing partner William Downey and I encountered unfishable conditions on a small trout stream. Since we had to cross a nice smallmouth river on the way home we decided to give it a try even though our tackle was very light. Fishing below one of these snow fence ledges William took an exceptionally large smallmouth. Since even small fish make a good showing on light tackle a large bass like this seems more like a tarpon.

Another type of water that holds sculpins and produces well is that portion of the river immediately adjacent to a bank made up of these large rocks. As with the last situation, flood waters dislodge many of these stones and distribute them right along the water's edge. If, under normal conditions, these areas are one to three feet deep and carry a moderate current we are in action. The sculpins are here and so are the bass.

I like to fish these banks by wading down the river a comfortable casting distance from the edge and casting my streamer straight in. Easy does it on the retrieve; the bass will often be within the first several feet of water. Get tight to your fly and be ready for a strike within the first several seconds.

William Downey fishing a Sculpin Streamer below a ledge where high water deposited grapefruit-sized rocks that formed ideal cover for minnows.

Use the same basic stripping action as before, and continue to fish the streamer out as far as the good bottom cover extends. In some cases you may not want to cover more than ten feet out from the bank; in other cases you may be able to pick up good fish for thirty feet. Some of these banks will be productive for hundreds of yards.

The mad tom—that brownish-blue minnow that looks like a baby catfish— is the number one bait for those seeking king-size smallmouth.

As with the sculpins, mad toms make their homes under rocks and like to stick close to the bottom most of the time. They may, however be found in slightly slower water. Recently I saw a youngster with a coffee can doing a pretty good job of catching them by turning over rocks in the shallow water at the side of the tail of a big pool.

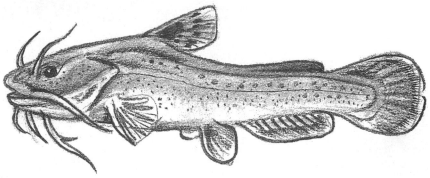

MAD TOM.
Mad Toms roam the stream to feed at night, so it is understandable why, "I have my best success fishing them during the first hour of daylight in the mornings."

Mad toms come out from under the rocks at night and move about the river to feed. When I was in high school we used to sell mad toms to the bait fishermen. It was an easy matter to seine ten dozen in several hours once it got dark.

My favorite streamers for imitating this minnow are Dave Whitlock's Hare Water Pup and Ed Shenk's Black Sculpin, both in sizes 2 to 8.

I have my best success fishing mad tom patterns for the first hour of daylight in the mornings. After foraging for food all night they seem to be a little slow getting back under their rocks and the bass get a good shot at them at this time.

Water about two or three feet deep over gravel bars can be very productive. These areas can be fished from either the river or the bank side. I like to cover these areas with a *very* slow stripping action, often wading upstream to avoid scaring the bass. I even like to feel the streamer bump the bottom occassionally just to let me know I'm getting it down to where the real ones are.

Heavily overcast days and slightly discolored water will often prompt the mad toms out into the open during daylight hours. This plus the fact that smallmouth generally like to feed heavily during these low light conditions tempts some anglers to go big-fish hunting.

WHITLOCK'S HARE WATER PUP.
Many nice fish can be caught on Whitlock's Hare Water Pup, fished over three-foot-deep gravel bars in low-light sitations.

Jeff Williamson fishing a Mad Tom fly pattern in slightly discolored water, which prompted the natural minnows to stay in open water.

It works. I know one smallmouth angler who, with amazing consistency, continues to catch very large smallmouth with mad tom patterns under these conditions. He knows his river well; knows the cover which holds good fish; knows where the mad toms make their homes and knows where the smallmouth go to look for them. The amazing part is that he catches larger bass from various parts of his river than most anglers realize would hold in that size water. Although this gentleman fishes only a few rivers, his understanding of smallmouth is so complete that I'm sure he would do well anywhere they are found.

With both the sculpins and the mad toms success depends on fishing the streamers close to the stream bottom. All the fly patterns discussed are tied with extra weight in the bodies to help achieve this. Depending upon the depth of the water and the speed of the current, we can often get the streamers down even with a floating line. Experimenting with casting at various angles across and up the currents, and with mending the line, will show you if you are getting your flies down properly. If you are not bumping the bottom occassionally with the streamer you are not doing it right.

When using a floating line it is best to use a leader about nine feet long with flies you want to fish deeply. This helps overcome the buoyancy of the floating line and gives the flies a better chance to reach the bottom.

Under certain circumstances it is advantageous to go to a sinking-tip fly line with sculpins and mad toms. If the water is more than five feet deep—or even less with a fast current—I find that I get much better results with these lines.

Sinking-tip lines are designed so the first ten feet sinks while the rest of the line floats. These are ideal for this streamer fishing because the sinking portion of the line takes the flies to the bottom while the floating part gives maximum control of the drift and strike detection.

High density sinking-tip lines do a better job than the slower sinkers. This is because we often need to get our streamers down quickly close to the riffles. Our flies would be out of the productive water if we had to wait a long time for the slower sinkers to do their jobs.

I do occasionally use a full thirty-foot-long high density sinking head for these bottom-bouncing flies in the spring when the streams are high. These lines do not afford the drift control that the sinking tip lines do, but if cabin fever gets you and you can't wait for the water to recede they are your best bet.

MID-WATER MINNOWS AND SWIMMING STREAMERS

Since we are attempting to "match the minnows" that smallmouth are accustomed to seeing, we would be remiss if we did not cover the chub minnows.

This robust silver-sided minnow is found in a variety of water types throughout most of the smallmouth's range. We find him in riffles, strong runs, rapids, heavy pockets and shoots. These minnows prefer moderately fast currents, but will often locate in the tails of pools possessing slower flows.

If you are an eastern trout fisherman you probably have had harsh words for this minnow, which will often hold in water fast enough for a rainbow trout and rise to a dry fly with all of a trout's enthusiasm.

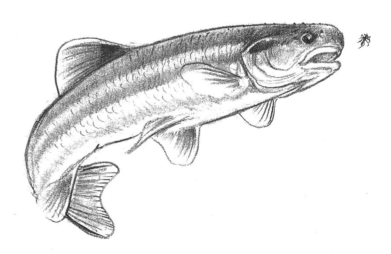

CHUB MINNOW.
This robust silver-sided minnow is found in a variety of water types throughout most of the smallmouth's range.

The two best streamers I have found for imitating chubs are Shenk's White Streamer and a White Zonker, with the former pattern being definitely preferred. Both are good in sizes four and six.

Although chub-type streamer fishing is one of the easiest forms of fishing for smallmouth—prompting me to use it when instructing Boy Scouts—the most consistent fishing will result from carefully reading the water.

Before fishing the riffle flowing into the head of a pool, identify those areas of maximum and minimum flow rates. Take note of sizeable underwater boulders and slightly deeper cuts in the stream bottom. Although these factors may be difficult to evaluate at first, experience will quickly provide you with an amazing understanding of how they affect the smallmouth. When feeding in these areas he will seek out slight breaks in the current that make it easier for him to hold his position, all the while keeping close to the fastest water.

One of the most productive and easily identified areas are the edges of riffle tongues, where fast water coming down a riffle meets slower water on one or

SHENK'S WHITE STREAMER. *Shenk's White Streamer just might be my overall favorite streamer; it is definitely the best chub imitation I've found. It is almost sure-fire when stripped along the edge of a riffle tongue.*

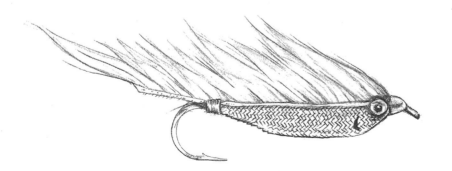

WHITE ZONKER. *The White Zonker is an effective streamer in areas holding chub minnows. The flash of its sides is an excellent attractor.*

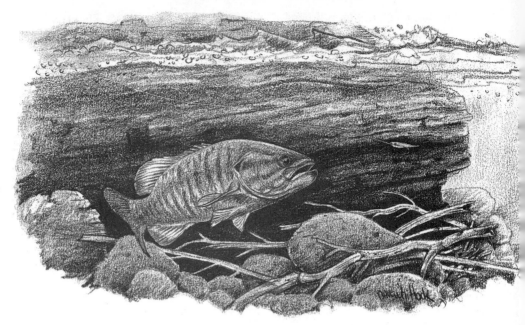

Before charging out to fish a stretch of water take time to read it. Note the sizeable underwater boulders and slightly deeper cuts in the stream bottom, which harbor bass.

both sides of the stream. This buffer area in itself gives the bass a perfect set up. He can hold in the slower water on the edge and easily grab any food coming down the main current. This area is usually created where the river gradually deepens as it slides along the edge of a gravel bar.

When fishing these areas I like to stay out toward the edge of the stream and cast my chub streamer across the slow water out about ten feet into the main current. Little streamer action is required since the current acts upon it so strongly. It is important to keep a tight line because the strike usually comes quickly right at the edge of the riffle tongue.

Even if I plan to fish the entire pool I like to first work this edge on down as far as it reaches in the pool. It is usually easy to pick up several smallmouth along the fast water–slow water juction. Wading on out into the pool first would spook these fish. Only after I've covered the edge do I work on the rest of the pool.

Back at the head of the pool, as we fish the main riffle with streamers, it is vital to pinpoint the holding areas mentioned earlier. Although one can always methodically cover the whole thing and pick up a few fish, but this hit-or-miss method will seldom get you anything but runts.

Swimming a Streamer

Identifying several large, submerged rocks in a stream not only gives us an idea of where a good bass should be, but more importantly it is our cue as to how to swim the streamer through that area to make it look alive. The idea is to cast the fly into a spot above and beyond the anticipated hot spot, and then *swim* it broadside by the bass on his feeding level, at a pace that will prompt him to strike it. It is fished broadside because it lets him see the streamer as a mouthful. If he is looking at it head or tail first, it may appear too small to excite him. We want it at his feeding level to make it easy for him to grab. If the bass is holding on the bottom in a pocket four feet deep and the streamer passes one foot below the surface he may not even know it's up there. Why take a chance?

The pace, or fishing speed, of the streamer must be slow enough to allow him to want to capture it. (He could catch it if it came racing by, but he may not want to.) On the other hand we do not want it moving too slowly: giving the bass too much time to examine the fly may let him detect it as a phony. It is better to give him just enough look at it to tempt him, yet have it moving fast enough to make him want to take it quickly before it gets away.

Fishing a chub imitation on down through the fastest parts of the pool will take lots of good fish. Remember, however, to read the water carefully so you can *swim your streamer* in a convincing manner.

Michael Fong, a very knowledgeable California angler and author, has written much helpful information on the effectiveness of swimming streamers.

I confronted a smallmouth situation several years ago which really shook me for two reasons. First, I could hardly believe this had been going on for all

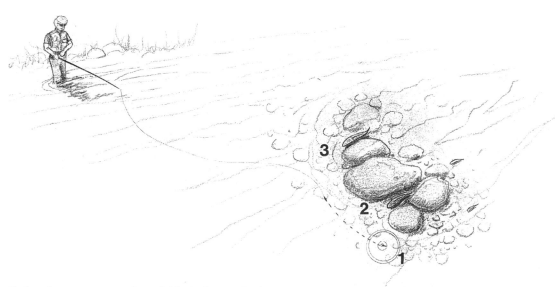

Swimming a streamer broadside in front of a bass is one of the most effective techniques to use with this type fly. First identify likely looking water, where there are sizeable submerged boulders in a moderate current three to four-feet deep. Cast your streamer to Point 1, above and beyond the hot spot, so it will have time to sink to the bass holding in areas 2 and 3. Carefully fish your streamer across in front of the bass at their levels.

of my life and I had been unaware of it. Second, I found it difficult to believe how many nice bass could be caught by taking advantage of it.

It all started one morning on a smallmouth river when the trico hatch was on (this is a small, size 22–24, black and white mayfly). I had fished this area hundreds of times before when these flies were hatching and had become accustomed to seeing the small bass feed upon them. These bass seldom ran even ten inches. I was in the mood to play with these small fish and put on a small dry fly. After catching a fair number of small bass I began thinking of all of this prime morning fishing time I was devoting to small fish. As I stood there thinking I saw the flashes of several large fish a foot or so under the water.

Even with the thick hatch of tricos I felt confident these fish were not taking the nymph of this fly. Sizeable smallmouth just don't seem interested in tiny flies. I had a size 4 Shenk's White Streamer on the drying pad on my vest and since I had no idea what the bass before me were feeding upon this seemed like as good a fly as any other.

I reworked my leader down to 2X and knotted on the Shenk's streamer. Casting it above the flashes I let the streamer drift back with just a gentle twitching action. The instant it entered the pocket I had a solid strike. It turned out to be a rather large smallmouth.

As I held him by the lip while removing my fly I noticed something sticking out of his throat. I pulled it out and noticed that it was a chub minnow which, lying there in my hand, looked almost like a photocopy of my Shenk's White Streamer. It was only at this point that I realized I had done what my old fishing tutor, Jack Sperry, had advised. Jack always said that if we wanted to be consistent in catching sizeable smallmouth we must duplicate what nature is doing.

Nature was cranking out the tricos by the thousands, and the chubs had moved in to feed on them, and the bass had moved in to feed on the chubs. Sounds simple, doesn't it? It is; that's why I wonder why it took me twenty years to notice it.

These flies start hatching in most smallmouth streams in mid-summer and continue until fall. During the first part of this period they start hatching about 7:00 AM and are on the water for about two hours. By September the flies may be as late as 10:00 AM before they start emerging but they will still be on for several hours. This can make for some very dependable action.

This fishing—for bass that are feeding on chubs that are feeding on tricos —may be found in a variety of water types throughout a stream. The only two areas I have *never* encountered it are where the water is too heavy for the minnows to hold and feed continously, and where the water is too shallow for the bass's comfort for extended periods.

I like to fish these set-ups by wading and fishing upstream with a size 4 or 6 Shenk's White Streamer—upstream because the bass will often be concentrated when feeding in this manner and I can pick off the downstream fish first without spooking the others. Cast the streamer just above the feeding minnows or flashing smallmouth and strip it back just slightly faster than the current.

William Downey fishing Shenk's White Streamer upstream into fish feeding actively on chubs working on a Trico hatch.

Some anglers using this strategy prefer to cast across stream into the feeding areas. Here the streamer is dropped just beyond the hot spot and stripped through it. This works very well; you just don't catch as many fish out of a given area since all that commotion either puts the others down or makes them move out.

This may be some of the fastest smallmouth fishing you will ever find—especially for large fish—so keep an eye out for it.

Before leaving the chubs there is one more fishing tactic to cover, what I call a "bounce retrieve." It consists of fishing the chub-type streamer (I still like the Shenk's White Streamer for this) almost straight upstream or up and across stream on a fairly short line. The weighted streamer is allowed to sink to the bottom, then is lifted about a foot and allowed to drift several feet and sink again. Repeat this for the full drift of the streamer. By combining a lifting action with the fly rod and stripping in the slack with the line hand we are able to create a bouncing action with the streamer.

Note that this is not the upstream, dead-drift fishing associated with nymphing. We do move the streamer—if only slightly—and impart this jigging action to it.

This technique makes the streamer look like an injured minnow drifting along the stream bottom, not quite in control and being pushed downstream by the current. Not only is this a very enticing action, but it simplifies strike detection. Since we will always have a tight line from the line hand down to the streamer we will both see and feel the strike.

This bounce retrieve can be handled nicely with a floating line, but even with a well weighted fly it may be necessary to use a split shot, or the mini sinking-head discussed earlier, on the leader.

How about a pattern which wasn't developed for bass, does not imitate a minnow, was named after a friend's high school colors, and catches smallmouth like crazy. Mix this with the fact that it is so simple that my eight-year-old daughter can tie it and it casts like a dream and you have a fly that sounds too good to be true.

This wonder fly is the James Wood Bucktail. It is so simple in appearance that it impresses no one. However, once they try it, it impresses everyone.

The smallmouth food which it is imitating, admittedly only in a vague suggestive manner, is the sunfish. If you did not think that smallmouth feed on sunfish, think again. Years ago, when they were considered legal baits, many of the local big-fish contests were won by fishermen using small bluegills as bait.

This pattern originated with Pete Perinchief, director of the Bermuda Fishing Information Bureau at Hamilton, Bermuda. Many years ago, when planning a bonefishing trip to Bermuda, I had written to Mr. Perinchief seeking information on what fly patterns I should tie. This was one of the flies. As it turned out I did not get to make the trip, so I had a lot of bonefish flies on hand. This was long before I owned a fly shop so I had no way to dispose of these flies. Finally— one of the luckiest moves I ever made—I decided to try them on smallmouth.

JAMES WOOD BUCKTAIL.
The James Wood Bucktail is so simple in appearance that you will probably not be impressed with it until you fish it, and the smallmouth let you know how great *they think it is.*

A streamer that resembles a sunfish, such as the James Wood Bucktail, usually produces well in shallow water around the grass.

Years later I presented this fly in one of my fly tying classes and referred to it as Perinchief's Bonefish Fly, but I told the fellows how great it was for smallmouth. One of the men, not really taken with its misplaced name, noted that it's basic blue and yellow colors were the same as his school colors—James Wood High School. The name stuck, and since that day hundreds of anglers have landed thousands of smallmouth on the James Wood Bucktail. It is very easy to tie, consisting of a fat blue chenille head and a yellow chenille body with a sparse white bucktail wrap-around wing.

This fly is productive anywhere smallmouth are accustomed to seeing sunfish. It is very effective in lakes along the shore, around islands, and over other shallow areas. These areas produce well in the spring with a floating line and I have done well later in the season with a James Wood Bucktail on a fast sinking-tip line in deeper water.

The same type of cover produces on rivers. In the spring the shallows are loaded with sunfish preparing to spawn so we can expect to do well then. By mid- to late summer the sunfish fry are large enough to attract the bass and we can do well again. There is no wrong time to fish this fly.

Sunfish are distributed so uniformly in many rivers that there really is no wrong place to fish this fly, either. They tend to avoid very strong currents but I have done well with this fly even in those areas. Sunfish are so thick in many streams that the bass know them well and will grab what they think is a helpless babe anytime they can.

No fancy fishing technique is needed here. You know how sunfish swim and that's what you want to duplicate. Experiment with the pace of the retrieve and use the one that works best.

MINNOWS IN THE SHALLOWS

The shallow areas of most smallmouth streams are loaded with the shiner-type minnows. Usually the greatest concentrations of them are found in and around aquatic grassbeds and on gravel bars over which the water can be anywhere from six inches to two feet deep.

These minnows have a very streamlined profile, a dark back, light bluish-green sides and silvery-white stomach. They are capable of moving very quickly, especially when pursued by a bass. When selecting streamers look for a pattern that duplicates both of these properties, matching the overall shape and coloration and capable of coming to life quickly in the water.

My favorite shiner imitations are Waterman's Silver Outcast and a White Marabou Muddler. I use the former most of the time since it best matches the overall shape and coloration of the shiner.

There are several ways to fish shiner waters, but lets look first at what I consider the most exciting.

SHINERS AND SILVER OUTCAST.
The shallows in many smallmouth waters are loaded with shiner-type minnows. Waterman's Silver Outcast streamer is the best pattern I've found in these waters; not only does it match the overall shape and coloration of the minnows, but it can be brought to life the instant it touches the water.

These minnows can be found around grassbeds and on shallow gravel bars all of the time, and the bass know it. However, most of this water is too shallow for the bass's comfort for extended periods. They prefer to visit these areas mainly when they feel a strong need to feed. This sets up what I call "the chase."

As the bass charge into the shallows for their meal the minnows flee, causing a commotion on the surface in their flight. You may see dozens of minnows swimming and splashing across ten feet of shallows for five seconds or so.

In fishing "the chase" I like to cast my streamer about five feet in front of and five feet beyond the escaping minnows. The instant it touches the water I bring it to life with a firm line-hand stripping action that moves the fly a foot on each quick strip. I am trying to bring the streamer across in front of the bass, making it easier to see and capture than the minnows racing away from him.

If I do not get a strike on the first cast I will immediately shoot the second and even third cast into the same area. If the third cast fails to yield a strike, experience has taught me that continuing to pound the water will usually put the bass down and he will not show again. It's better to retrieve the fly and wait until the chase commences again. Usually the bass will surface within a few minutes in the same general area. This time I am ready and I can shoot my fly right on target. I take more fish on the second chase than I do on the first.

If the bass comes up out of range the second or third time, don't try to race to the area quickly while he's on the minnows. You'll seldom make it in time, and the commotion you'll make on the way will probably put the fish down for good. There's a better way. (In fact this is the way I normally fish these areas early and late in the day when I know there is a good chance of seeing a "chase.")

I wade up or down the river within comfortable casting distances of the shallows. I fish the water as usual but with a pattern like the Silver Outcast that will pass for these shiners. I keep all the line off of the reel that I can shoot with one back cast, ready for the bass when he shows. At that instant I pick up my fly and fire it at him.

If fishing the chase doesn't get you excited, you had better go back to golf.

Although chases most often happen early and late in the day these are not the only times they can occur. During a slide show one morning in a recent smallmouth fly-fishing school I had discribed this situation and suggested that the students keep an eye out for it while fishing that evening. As it turned out they did not have to wait that long: when we got on the river about 11:00 AM there were bass chasing minnows everywhere. The day was heavily overcast and the smallmouth were comfortable in water hardly deep enough to cover them, feeling no need to wait until evening to cash in on the shiners.

Tadpoles

Another minnow (if we can call him that) found in the shallows in large numbers is the tadpole. We don't hear much about this babe of the frog, but the bass know him well.

The cover that attracts the tadpole is quite different from what shiners call home. Tadpoles like a very slow current and a mud bottom. When frightened they dive into the mud to hide.

Although not tied to pass for a tadpole, my favorite streamer here is Shenk's Black Sculpin in sizes 4 to 8.

As with the shiners, the smallmouth usually dash out onto the shallows, grab a few, and return to the comfort of deeper water close by. Realizing this, I often catch some nice fish by casting the streamer out onto these flats and then easing it off into the deeper water. The strike usually comes just as the fly leaves the shelf and drops off. Often the bass are lying there just waiting for a tadpole to make this move.

The author casting a shiner-type streamer in front of a smallmouth chasing minnows in shallow water close to the bank.

WOUNDED MINNOWS AND SHALLOW SWIMMERS

Often, especially in low water conditions, smallmouth go for streamers fished just under the surface. Since this is not a normal way for minnows to swim I can only assume the bass take them as wounded or dying minnows. We don't see many real minnows struggling along the surface because they don't last long there before being eaten. I've seen them grabbed often enough to be convinced the bass are aware they have an easy meal. This comes close to surface fishing with top-water bugs, but sometimes one is more effective than the other. I use both.

One August evening Bill Burslem and I took our young sons camping along the river. The boys wanted to play around camp so Bill and I decided to fish even though the river was extremely low. Not knowing exactly where we would fish I tied on a White Marabou Muddler. Since we were running out of light we both decided to start at the same riffle. Bill fished downstream and I fished up.

The tail of the pool I was fishing was slow and flat with few areas over two feet deep. There were a few deeper cuts between some ledges and on the far bank. My White Marabou Muddler was not weighted, but to help keep it off the bottom I greased the deer hair head with silicone cream. I was pleasantly surprised at the number of fish I picked up in that low water as I worked my way upstream. None of these fish were real large but they came in good numbers and were lots of fun.

I have experimented a lot with these shallow tails since then, and have found that many of them produce well in low water when fished upstream with shallow swimming streamers. In addition to the unweighted Marabou Muddlers, the Dahlberg Diving Minnows and Flashdancers are also effective as shallow swimmers.

Lefty Kreh stripping a wounded-minnow-type streamer just under the surface in some broken water below a riffle.

The basic technique for fishing pool-tails is to cast the streamers up and across stream and apply a firm, six-inch strip with the line hand to dive the fly under. Then when it bounces back to the top strip the line in just fast enough to keep up with its natural rate of drift. Let it ride for three or four feet then dive it under again. Keep repeating this all the way back.

A similar technique that works in these shallow tails employs a continuous line-hand twisting retrieve. Here I move the streamer slightly faster than the current so it wiggles and rolls on the surface.

The heads of the pools if they are less than four feet deep and not too fast can often be fished successfully with shallow swimming streamers.

Since we usually fish these heads below the riffles by casting down and across stream the retrieve is slightly different. Here it's more of a dive-swing-dive procedure with the speed and lengths of the stripping varied to meet the stream conditions and desires of the bass.

7

Smallmouth Nymphing

Nymphing is my favorite form of smallmouth fishing, and the system I turn to when things get tough. It is also the form most of the serious anglers in my schools want to learn more about, for the simple reason that it works. If you're skillful enough, it can be better than *any* other system.

Nymphing for smallmouth is the author's favorite tactic.

Charley Waterman admires a nice smallmouth that took a Murray's Hellgrammite fished dead drift in a riffle. Photo by Charles F. Waterman.

DEAD-DRIFT NYMPHING

Let's start with the most difficult form of nymphing first—dead drift nymph fishing. This means casting and fishing the nymph upstream, letting it drift back downstream at about the same speed as the current.

With this approach we can get our flies deeper, while still using a floating line, than we can with any other type of presentation. Obviously the closer to straight up the current we can cast, the better depth we will achieve. Casting up and across at a ten- to twenty-degree angle is about as far to the side as you can deviate and still expect to get the fly down in very fast water.

This technique calls for fishing a short line. Casts over thirty feet will seldom allow you to get the depth you need and, if you do get down deep and a strike comes, you will seldom realize it in time to set the hook.

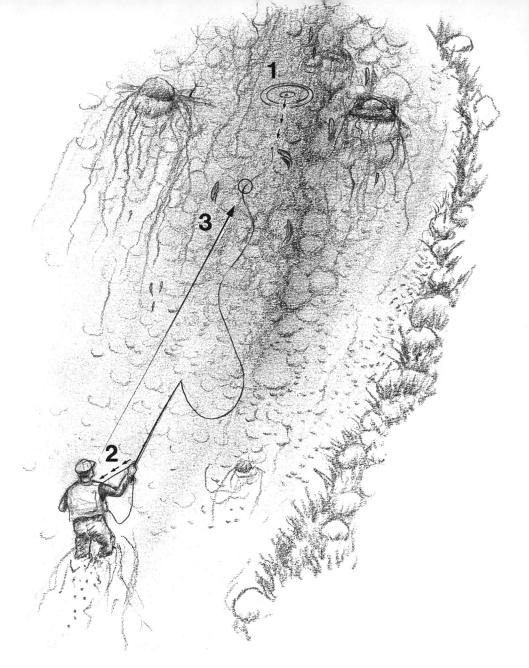

Upstream nymphing technique.

Upstream dead-drift nymphing is extremely effective, but the strike must be seen *rather than felt.*

Step 1: *Presentation of nymph thirty feet upstream.*

Step 2: *As the nymph sinks and drifts downstream, the slack line is retrieved with the line hand.*

Step 3: *Angler watches the indicator closely in order to detect the strike.*

That's the second problem in this approach—detecting the strike. I often hear the comment "I felt the strike, but I couldn't hook him." If you are unaware of the strike until you feel it, you won't hook many smallmouth with this technique. You should *see* the strike in dead drift nymphing before you feel it. By the time you feel the strike the line has already come tight and the bass, feeling the resistance on the line and the phony nymph, has started rejecting the fly. Realizing that it takes only 1½ to 2 seconds for the fish to reject the fly, you can see your chances of hooking him have greatly reduced.

Start preparing to detect the strike as the line completes its turnover in the air. At this point, use the line hand to place the fly line under the first or second finger of the rod hand. If it is apparent that there will be any slack in the fly line as it settles to the water—and most of the time there is—remove the slack by stripping it in over a rod finger with the line hand. Fail to do this and you are playing a catch-up game from the time your nymph enters the water. In very fast water, you may never catch up. Without a tight line from the line hand to the nymph you will be unable to detect the strike in time to set the hook.

Since we must see the strike, what do we look for? Refer back to the "strike detecting system," covered in Chapter 1 under Leaders. This leader system, consisting of bright fluorescent mono in the butt and mid sections with several indicators, is the greatest aid I've ever found in nymphing.

I always watch the part of this leader system closest to the fly. If my first indicator is three feet above the fly and I can see it, that's what I watch. If the fly is so deep that I cannot see this I watch the second one. If I am unable to see either one, I watch the bright butt of the leader. If none of this is visible I am compelled to watch the line–leader connection, but since this junction is so far from the nymph I usually miss strikes by relying upon it. It is better to wade into a casting position that will let you work with a shorter line.

I was once working with a very capable angler who wanted to learn more about nymph fishing. We were in a run I knew was loaded with smallmouth, but he couldn't seem to score. I was standing right at his elbow and couldn't see what he was doing wrong. Finally in frustration he shoved the rod over to me saying, "You try it." I took the rod, still with the line on the water, and made one cast up into the area he had been fishing. Right away I thought I knew the problem. I cranked five feet of line back onto the reel, handed the outfit back and asked him to move upstream five feet closer to the target. Bang, bang, bang—he caught several nice smallmouth without moving out of his tracks. He had been getting the strikes all along but had so much line on the water that neither one of us could see them. The line–leader connection is an adequate indicator only in slower water.

You've got to use some judgment here. The closer you get to the bass the better your chances of detecting the strikes, but the greater your chances of spooking them. Staying further back you won't spook them, but you may not detect the strike, either. It's a trade-off that must be made in every area you fish. Judging it right requires reading the water carefully.

The author fishing his Hellgrammite Fly upstream dead drift. Watching the indicators or fluorescent leader butt is a great aid in strike detection here.

The first step in reading the water for smallmouth nymphing is to identify where the bass will be holding. Since we are still talking about upstream dead-drift nymph fishing, the second step is to select the proper spot upstream as the target. The third step is to determine where to stand to make the presentation.

Many anglers go about this backwards and voice the opinion that "this riffle must be fished out" as they stand where they should be fishing after fishing where they should have been standing.

Let's assume you've correctly identified where the fish should be, know where to drop your nymph, and you're in a spot to put it all together. You cast about twenty-five feet upstream. The first six or eight feet of the drift is used mainly to get the nymph to the bottom. The next six or eight feet of the drift is used to get the fly under complete control so it is going where you want it and so you will be able to detect the strike when it comes. This means you are actually fishing the nymph for only about ten feet. That's right, ten feet—but be patient. With practice, this technique will become amazingly effective.

Some anglers develop such a keen sixth sense at this game that they find themselves setting the hooks on nice bass without consciously knowing what triggered their reflex to strike the fish.

Dead-drifting nymphs, as with the next system we are going to cover, is exceptionally productive in water containing hellgrammites and stoneflies. The best three patterns I know for these are the Murray's Hellgrammite, which Ron Kommer is primarily responsible for, Charlie Brooks' Dark Stonefly Nymph, and the Bitch Creek Nymph, all in sizes 8 to 4.

ARTIFICIAL NYMPHS.
Top, *Murray's Hellgrammite;* lower left, *Bitch Creek Nymph;* lower right, *Brooks's Dark Stonefly Nymph. Smallmouth bass are accustomed to feeding on large natural nymphs, and drifting one of these fly patterns by them will usually induce a strike.*

SWING NYMPHING

The "swing system" of nymph fishing is much easier to learn than the dead-drift system, less demanding in timing, water reading, and strike detection. Why not use this all the time? There are some places dead drifting is more productive—but the converse is also true.

Let's look at an example of water that is ideally fished by "swing nymphing."

We're standing on the left side of a large river looking upstream. Thirty feet upstream is a fast riffle which dumps its water quickly into a pool in front of us eight feet deep. This is not a gentle pool, for the water rushes through it quite fast. Only the fact that it is 200 feet wide and 100 feet long prompts me to call it a pool.

The pool is too deep to wade for dead-drift nymphing and the water is moving so fast that a streamer fished across it would be snapped out long before it could reach the bottom. Enter "swing nymphing."

The technique requires that we stand approximately even with the area we plan to fish. Since we will be able to cover the water from fifteen to forty feet out from where we are there is no need to move very far out into the pool yet. A nymph (the hellgrammite just mentioned is perfect) is cast as far up into the riffle as we can get it without hanging there. Logically we should cover the water closest to us first so the fly is cast so it will drift back about fifteen feet out from our position.

Absolutely no line is recovered until we estimate that the nymph is about five feet upstream. Remember, *don't strip that line.* The only thing we want to do up to this point is hold the excess slack line off of the water with an extended arm and rod. We are simply trying to let the nymph sink as deep as it can. Any action on our part up to now will pull it up off of the bottom. Once it gets deep, and is just upstream of our position and fifteen feet out, tighten up with the line hand until you can feel the nymph. In many cases you can actually feel it bumping the bottom.

Invariably we will be fishing across some fast water so it is important to reach up and out as far as you can with your fly rod at a 45-degree angle. This is also the perfect position for fishing the nymph. Once you are tight to it, do not use the line hand to retrieve more line. Fish the nymph by swinging the rod at the same rate that the current is pushing the nymph. We are actually fishing the water from just above us (fifteen feet out) to about twenty feet below us, and the nymph is drifting along the bottom all of the way.

Since we are tight to the nymph with the swinging rod the strike is simultaneously felt and seen. However, with the depth we now have and the belly in the line it is important that we strike the fish fast and hard with both the line hand and the rod.

This first cast ran the fly only fifteen feet out. In order to cover more water

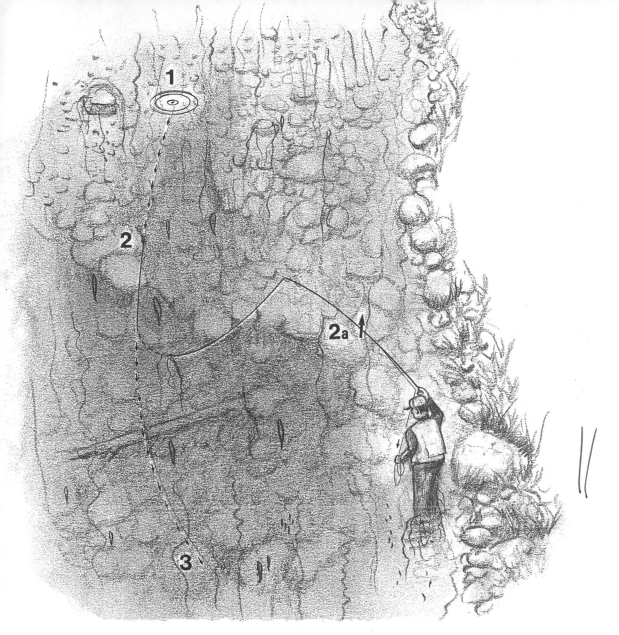

"Swing nymphing" will enable you to fish your nymphs more effectively in deeper runs and pockets than any other technique.

Step 1: *Presentation of nymph upstream.*

Step 2: *Nymph sinks on a slack line and drifts downstream naturally.*

Step 2A: *Some slack is pulled in with the line hand and rod is raised to maintain contact with the nymph.*

Step 3: *Angler pivots, and with the rod extended up and out, in order to bridge any fast currents, fishes the nymph to a downstream position.*

Dick Rabun used the swing-nymphing technique to hook this bass on a deeply fished nymph.

just cast a little further out on the next shot—still dropping your nymph just below the riffle. By gradually lengthening your casts you can comfortably cover the water out to about forty feet from this position.

If you can wade out further naturally you can cover more of the pool. But trying to effectively cover the water fifty to seventy feet out with this technique is not the best idea. Casting is no problem but controlling the drift becomes haphazard.

Swing nymphing is very effective on any deep pool regardless of the size, as long as you have room to drop your nymph far enough above the bass to give it time to sink.

This system is very much like the technique the late Charlie Brooks taught me long ago on the Madison River fishing for large trout. Although Brooks used a thirty-foot, fast-sinking head while we use a floating line, and there are a few more subtle differences, if you can handle Brooks' system you can handle this.

When using either the dead-drifting system or the swinging system don't be afraid to move the nymph slightly faster than the current for short periods. Both the stoneflies and the hellgrammites are good swimmers, and the bass are accustomed to seeing them move about the stream. Be careful not to overdo this since it will deprive you of some depth, but there are times when this is not a serious problem.

In certain situations we can fish hellgrammite and stonefly nymph patterns across and downstream with excellent results—cranefly and general nymph patterns like the Casual Dress work well here also.

Basically these will be portions of the stream such as moderate riffles and generally well aerated water where the natural nymphs are found, but which are not very swift or deep. I can't express this in numbers for the flow rate and depth, but you'll know.

If you fish a riffle or run down and across and don't come out with anything but small bass you probably aren't getting adequate depth. You may be in nursery water which holds only these small fish, although even moderately fast riffles and runs which hold large bass will have their share of small fish. These are the fish we catch with inadequate nymph depth. The larger fish instinctively know better than to fight their way up through four feet of fast water to take a two-inch nymph.

The technique for fishing these nymphs across and downstream is much like some of our streamer methods. The cast is made across the current and worked very slowly as the current swings it downstream. Mending is often required in order to keep the nymphs close to the bottom. Since it is only logical that we would fish a longer line here it is important that we keep a tight line all the way to the nymph so we can feel the strike.

DRAGONFLY AND DAMSELFLY NYMPHS

In slightly slower water Dragonfly Nymphs and Damselfly Nymphs can be very effective in this across-stream presentation.

With these two patterns it is often advantageous to impart a short, brisk stripping action during the retrieve. The natural nymphs move along the stream bottom with a short, jet-like spurting action as they feed, and this is what we want to duplicate. At other times a slow, line-hand twisting action is most productive, so experiment.

Keep in mind that most of the action will come when the nymphs are worked close to the stream bottom.

If the current is not very fast and the water is not over five feet deep, it is normally possible to gain adequate depth with a nine-foot leader on a floating line. However, some deeper areas produce better with a sinking-tip line.

Damselfly nymphs are extremely effective around aquatic grassbeds, brush piles, and partly submerged tree tops. The nymphs use these as ladders for gaining access to the stream surface where they pop their wings and become adult flies. This brisk activity continues all summer and smallmouth take advantage of it.

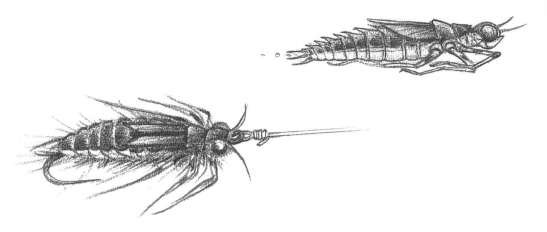

Dragonfly patterns are most effectively fished in a darting manner, close to the stream bottom.

One exceptionally large smallmouth I named Patch made his home in a relatively small area right beside a patch (hence his name) of aquatic grass. I caught Patch off and on for several years with the score greatly in his favor. Although one might assume that he was rather large to feed on something as delicate as damselfly nymphs, he definitely had a weakness for them. Maybe he just liked the taste.

There are several ways to fish Damselfly Nymphs around grassbeds and brush. The same across stream technique we've been discussing works well. If the area you are fishing is fairly shallow it is wise to fish a long line to avoid scaring the bass.

Drop your nymph in close to the cover and use a slow-strip, darting action. The bass are accustomed to seeing the naturals close to the grass so don't be in a hurry to strip your fly out into open water. Most strikes will come within ten feet of the cover.

A second method of fishing Damselfly Nymphs around grassbeds is to approach these beds from the downstream side and cast straight up to them. I prefer this system because there is less chance of scaring the fish. This becomes especially significant in late summer and in the fall as the water level drops and the grassbeds grow to their fullest.

8

Strymphs: The Crossbreed

Hitting the stream shortly after daylight I decided to fish a heavy riffle that I knew held lots of sculpin minnows. Casting across and downstream I took a fair number of fish with conventional streamer tactics.

After covering the riffle I had only about a half an hour left before I had to get to work. This wasn't enough time to go anywhere else, so I decided to fish the lower part of the pool running into the riffle. This was not one of those shallow, fast tails. The water ran from waist- to chest-deep and was fairly slow—typical dragonfly nymph water. Using the same fly I fished this water up and across stream, working the fly along the bottom with a darting action much the way real dragonflies move. This water also yielded some nice smallmouth.

The fly? A Black Strymph. How could the same fly pass for a sculpin in the riffle and a dragonfly nymph in the slow water? Because it has the suggestive look of, and can be made to fish like, both of these food forms.

The Strymphs were the outcome of several years of trial-and-error fishing. I wanted a fly which would pass for both the streamer and the nymph, and would cover a variety of needs.

To arrive at a workable fly pattern I adapted a system from Vince Marinaro, who had recently developed his ''game of nods'' for devising flies for the fussy brown trout on the Letort. In his attempt to develop flies when existing patterns were inadequate, Vince would fish several slightly different flies over fish he could see. The selective fish would come up to investigate the flies but refuse to take them. The number of ''look-rises'' each pattern received were counted as positive nods. In order to develop a workable pattern Vince would take parts from the flies receiving the greatest number of nods and incorporate them into one fly.

I did somewhat the same thing. I selected about a dozen of our best streamers

135

STRYMPH

The bass voted for the components used in constructing this unusual fly. It is very effective when fished as either a streamer or a nymph.

and a dozen of our best nymphs and started interchanging various parts as I tied them. Since I was unable to watch the smallmouth's reactions to the various test flies I decided to fish each one an equal amount of time on water of equal quality. I kept records of the number of fish caught on each test fly.

For several seasons I continued to cross streamers and nymphs. Some of the flies were very unusual in appearance but caught a fair number of fish. Others looked great but caught nothing. This testing was a lot of fun and a real eye-opener on the preferences of smallmouth.

The winner, by a considerable margin, was a pattern utilizing the body style of Shenk's Streamers and the tail of Murray's Hellgrammite.

The chewy fur body of Shenk's Streamers proved every bit as productive from a nymph point of view as it had always been on his White Streamer and Black Sculpin. The ostrich herl, when used as a streamer wing or tail, did the job as well here as it had on my Hellgrammite for the past fifteen years.

The Black Strymph was the original pattern. When fished as a nymph it took bass in waters which contained natural hellgrammites, dark stonefly nymphs, and dragonfly nymphs. When fished as a streamer in waters where mad toms, sculpins, and tadpoles lived it was outstanding—being on a par with the best of these patterns.

Admittedly the Black Strymph is only mildly suggestive in appearance of these specific food forms, but it can be fished like them convincingly.

Since I was striving to imitate a broad variety of minnows and nymphs I decided to try the same style of tie in a cream color. This proved very effective in and below riffles where chubs were located. Fishing it down and across stream it was about equal with Shenk's White Streamer. This was predictable since the body and overall shape are so similar. However, one feature enabled it to become one of the best flies of all times for fishing it as a minnow imitation upstream with the bounce retrieve.

When ostrich herl gets wet the strong stem fibers have a great affinity for each other. This enables the tail of this fly to wiggle as one solid unit if the current above it suddenly pushes it faster than the retrieve. For this reason, I use it more and more when I want to fish upstream in the fast water from just below a riffle on up into the riffle itself.

In addition to mistaking it for a chub in these fast-water areas, the smallmouth may think it is a cranefly or caddis larva or a large mayfly nymph, which also make their homes here.

The Olive Strymph was added to further broaden the potential areas in which this pattern could be used. This is one of the most productive flies in areas where damselflies and dragonflies are found. It's capacity for being fished either upstream or down with equal effeciency simplifies the decision on the best way to approach areas holding these nymphs—you can suit yourself.

This pattern is also outstanding in trout spring creeks where these two nymphs are found—but that's another story. I'll only mention that, several weeks after teaching the tying of this fly in one of my classes, one of the students landed two rainbows over five pounds in one day on a spring creek.

This olive pattern works well as a streamer where shiner minnows are found. Normally we tie this fly weighted, so naturally it would not work well in the shallows when the bass are chasing minnows. However, it does a good job when fished right where these shallow sections of the river meet deeper water.

Bass are accustomed to feeding on shiners here as they stray too far from home. Stay out in the river and fish the Olive Strymph across a gravel bar out into the deeper water with a medium stripping action.

Some sculpin minnows have a definite olive color so we are not out of line when using this fly in faster water areas where they make their homes. For whatever reason, the Olive Strymph has become one of the most popular patterns I sell.

Recently, after doing a slide show on smallmouth for the Federation of Fly Fishers National Conclave, I heard lots of good stories about the Strymphs. Anglers from all across the country came up to tell me of the outstanding success they had had with these flies in various conditions.

Still, I do not see this as a fly to replace all other smallmouth flies. There never will be such a fly. Even if there were, it would take a lot of the fun out of this game.

The most productive sizes for the Strymphs are sizes 4 through 8 in all three

Jeff Williamson is fishing his Olive Murray's Strymph upstream around grass in hopes the fish will take it as a damselfly nymph—but he may shoot the next cast across-stream and fish it like a minnow.

colors. If you are tying your own (I'll tell you how in Chapter 12) you can expand their potential by varying the amount of lead you put on under the body. You may want to tie several unweighted for use in the shallows while adding extra lead for bottom bouncers.

STRYMPH AND FOOD MATCHING CHART

Fly	*Nymphs*	*Minnows*
Black Strymph	Hellgrammite	Sculpin
	Dark Stonefly	Mad Tom
	Dragonfly	Tadpole
	Leech	
Olive Strymph	Damselfly	Sculpin
	Mayfly	Shiner
	Caddis Larva	
Cream Strymph	Cranefly Larva	Chub
	Mayfly	Silverside
	Caddis Larva	Shad
		Shiner

9

The Leech and Crawfish

Most people do not consider leeches very attractive and prefer having very little to do with them. Smallmouth have a different set of values and feed heavily upon them anytime they can.

Leeches are present in the slow to medium current sections of rivers where silt or rubble bottoms exist, and in many of lakes. The most common leech colors are dark brown, dark olive, and grayish black.

Leeches swim with a pronounced undulating action that we should strive to imitate with our flies. Their natural rate of swimming varies considerably, but most often they move about much slower than minnows. Considering this, and the fact that they are usually close to the stream bottom, we need to choose imitations carefully.

Leeches swim with a pronounced undulating action that we should strive to imitate with our flies.

140

Again, a primary factor in fly selection is the ability of the pattern to "fish right." We must be able to make it swim in a manner resembling the real leech, especially to take the larger fish. I feel this "fishability" is more important in leech patterns than the actual appearance of the fly.

My favorite leech pattern is the Black Fur or Bunny Leech in sizes 4 and 6. This is a very simple pattern which is tied like Charlie Brooks' Assam Dragon, where a strip of fur, on the hide, is wrapped on the hook shank. Here it is also allowed to extend loosely beyond the bend of the hook.

This is a very effective leech pattern. Much of its appeal rests in the fact that we can make it look alive with very little manipulation (an important attribute of any fly which will be fished deep and slowly). The loose fur on this fly is so alive in the water that you could not make it lie still.

Woolly Buggers and Flash-A-Buggers with all-black or black-and-olive bodies in sizes 4 through 8 are also good leech patterns.

Several years ago I fished a river that was close to its all-time low water level. It was mid-October and there had been almost no rain since May. The aquatic grassbeds pushed all the way to the water's surface in what had been the deepest pools.

Because the waters I usually fished were too shallow, I was compelled to fish some of these pools. Most of the water ranged from waist- to shoulder-deep, a perfect set up for getting in over your waders.

The water was so clear I could see the bottom no matter how deep I waded. Finally I fished myself into a spot from which it was too deep to move into any new water. Since I had been picking up a few fish all along, I was reluctant to backtrack. I was pretty sure I'd spooked most of the slow area I'd waded through.

I decided to stay where I was and cover all the water thoroughly that I could reach from that spot before wading back to the bank and going elsewhere. Since I had waded up and across stream to reach this spot I was most interested in the water further up that had not been fished. As it happened I was standing right at the far downstream end of a grassbed about fifty feet wide that reached up the river about 100 feet.

I continued to use the deer-hair surface bug I had been fishing and took about eight more fish, but finally I had covered all of the water I could reach and the action stopped. Wanting to milk all of the action I could get from that area before moving, I decided to fish underwater. The Fur Leech was a logical choice; there were plenty of real leeches in this water and the pattern lends itself well to a slow, deep retrieve. Methodically I started covering the water out beyond the grassbed and swimming the streamer all the way back in with a slow, line-hand twisting retrieve. Although this happened several years ago it stands out vividly in my mind because of all of the fish I landed on that leech without moving out of my tracks. I won't quote numbers, but let's say lots. Looking back on this incident I realize there were many things working in my favor that I had not recognized at the time.

Wading deep and working a fur leech slowly across the stream bottom is an excellent way to catch big bass.

First, the low water conditions had caused the bass to concentrate on the water that was left. Since the water temperature had started to drop as fall approached this also told them to look for the deeper water. The cooler water also slowed down the smallmouth's metabolism, and they did not need as much food, nor were they willing to move as far for it as they were earlier in the season. Although this good fishing came about almost by accident, I now stay alert for similar situations each fall, and have actually taken advantage of it dozens of times.

Under certain conditions the bass prefer an exaggerated retrieve which resembles the undulating, swimming motion of the leech. I encounter this most often in areas with a medium speed current. Leeches are seldom found in the riffles in the concentrations in which they are found in the slower areas, but will often be in water just a hundred feet or so below riffles.

Here a short bounce retrieve is ideal. By casting up and across stream with not over forty feet of line we can impart this undulating action quite convincingly. The fly is allowed to sink to the bottom. Then as it drifts downstream with the current we lift the fly rod to about 45 degrees and then drop it back, repeating this about every five feet of the drift. It is very important to use the line hand to take up any slack in order to stay tight to the fly as it settles back to the bottom. Without this we would not be aware of the strike when it comes.

It is often beneficial to experiment back and forth between this jigging bounce retrieve and a more uniform steady retrieve. Mixing these up, even in the same water, is a good way to find just what the bass want under those specific conditions.

There are certain conditions under which the leeches are more active and readily available to the fish than others. One sunny morning I was fishing with a good friend, and we had picked up a fair number of fish on a variety of flies but were not setting any records. Just before noon a very thick cloud cover moved in. It got very dark—looking more like late evening than mid-day.

Soon I heard my friend call and looked downstream to see him fighting a very large fish. He had no more than landed that fish until he was onto another one. My curiosity got to me so I went down to see what he was using. ''A leech,'' he said, ''they come out and move about more in low light situations.'' He sure proved his point!

Anytime we encounter low light conditions we should consider leech patterns. This could be late evening, heavily overcast days, or slightly discolored water. Some rich lakes have such great leech populations that many anglers feel it is foolish to waste time fishing any patterns except leeches.

I'm not sure I'd go that far, but leech patterns will take a lot of nice fish under these conditions.

CRAWFISH

Studies have shown that crawfish rank very high on the food list of smallmouth bass. I had never questioned this since some of this work was conducted by very knowledgeable professionals, one of whom was Ben Schley, a good friend and first-class angler. However, many years ago I had a real eye-opener on this point. I was fishing along a good smallmouth river and came upon two fellows seining bait in shallow water. Just to make conversation, and to see how much of the various foods were available, I stopped and talked to them a while. They were seining for crawfish and easily catching a fair number. It turned out that they were camped close by and had been fishing here for several days.

Upon their insistence I followed them to their camper to see some of the ''big fish'' they had caught on crawfish. How many times have you heard that story? When they popped the lid on their ice chest I could hardly believe my eyes. They had more big bass there than I had caught in the whole season. Needless to say, I could hardly wait to get back over to the river and put on a crawfish pattern. I did—and took a number of nice fish.

There are a number of crawfish flies on the market developed by such knowledgeable anglers as Dave Whitlock, Ben Schley, Bob Clouser, and Dave McCormick. All of these are good in sizes 8 to 4.

Crawfish are an important part of the smallmouth's diet in many waters. The imitation should be fished along the stream bottom with a darting action.

Before tying or buying a crawfish imitation, some research by the late Charlie Brooks is worth considering. Through diligent underwater observations Brooks concluded that flies with greatly contrasting back and belly colorations, or any other characteristics that enabled the fish to detect a "wobble," were less productive than flies tied, as he called it, "in the round."

Brooks told me that when a leader, played upon by the current, pulls the fly along it causes it to turn back and forth sideways in a wobbling manner. Brooks said that he had seen fish about to strike a fly actually swerve away if a wobble was apparent. His explanation for this behavior by the fish was that the natural nymphs and crawfish never acted in this manner. Brooks also noted that the deeper the flies were fished the more often this undesirable action occurred. This was logical since the current had a much greater chance to act upon the leader and wobble the fly.

These facts tell us several things about selecting and fishing crawfish flies. Basically, the more exaggerated the pincers are on a fly (and thus move "out of round,") the quicker we will get into trouble. Some of the most productive ties are those with sparsely tied pincers and those tied so the pincers extend straight back rather than sharply out to the sides.

This "wobble factor" also accounts for why we often do better fishing a crawfish pattern in shallow waters where the current does not get as much time to pull the leader and adversely affect the fly action.

Crawfish make their homes in tunnel-like dens on the stream bottom under large rocks and logs, and along the edges of aquatic grassbeds. In most cases they do not like very deep water. Like the leech, the crawfish is most active in low-light situations, coming out of its den to feed late in the evening and at night.

Under normal conditions crawfish crawl forward over the stream bottom, but when they find themselves in danger—such as being pursued by a bass—they flee backwards. Using their powerful tails like flippers they swim with a fast, darting action from one area of cover to the next. Since we are trying to "duplicate nature" these last three characteristics say a lot about when, where, and how to fish crawfish flies. This works out to fishing the fly with a firm, stripping action, close to the bottom over shallow rubble late in the day. This is by no means the only way to fish a crawfish, but the more of these properties you put into practice, the better fishing you will have.

10

River Fishing from a Canoe or Boat

Smallmouth float trips have a nostalgic quality; As I read his outstanding book *Fresh-water Bass* I can easily picture Ray Bergman with his wife and guide fishing down the beautiful Ozark streams fifty years ago. The fishing was great and the overall experience very rewarding.

Float fishing for smallmouth can be just as good today as it was then. Although dams have destroyed some once great bass rivers, there remain many excellent streams that lend themselves well to floating.

Float trips can be as complicated as you want to make them. Some people make elaborate plans for trips of several weeks, juggling cars, tents, cooking equipment, food, and tackle, making an African safari look like childs' play. Others enjoy covering only a mile or two in the evening after work.

The logistics are fairly simple. If two people are floating together one car is spotted at the take-out point and one is used to put the canoe in upstream. (Throughout this chapter I will be using the word "canoe," but the same comments apply to boats.) If only one vehicle is suitable for hauling the canoe it is best to drop the canoe off upstream and then spot this vehicle at the take-out point. This takes a little more time when you are starting out, but it simplifies things at the end of the trip: if you take longer on the float than anticipated and end up floating to your car in the dark, or if bad weather hits and you decide to paddle on through to the car, this simplifies things.

The easiest way to arrange getting in and out on a float trip is to have someone drop you off and then pick you up at a designated time and spot downstream. But this scheme has its hazards. One day my son and I used this system, planning for my wife to pick us up downstream eight hours later. The weather in the morning was beautiful, but at midafternoon a severe thunderstorm hit. There was too much lightning to stay on the river so we beached the canoe

The author uses a canoe to reach remote stretches of rivers, which receive little angling pressure.

and took cover. This was a questionable call since there was nothing but solid forest on both sides of the river. Strong winds came up and we had trees—not limbs, but trees—falling everywhere. Fortunately we made it through all of this safely and finally floated on to the designated pickup spot at the specified time. If I had left my Jeep at the take-out spot I would have paddled on through when I saw the storm coming and avoided the whole ordeal.

In addition to enjoying the scenery and seeing the wildlife, there are many advantages to float trips. It is an excellent way to get to water that receives a minimum of angling pressure, getting you to water far away from roads, or to water lying within fenced or private land. There are also many areas that afford excellent angling around islands in midstream surrounded by water too deep to wade.

Many anglers like to take float trips spanning several days and camp in tents overnight along the way. This is a lot of fun and lets you fish a broad variety of water. It is wise to plan your camping location ahead of time in order to be sure you have a safe, legal spot for the night. There are many canoe camping areas on National Forest land and even some on private land. Some state Fish and Game Agencies have maps showing access and camping areas. Most National Forest Service regional offices have maps of their lands that show campgrounds.

One word of caution: if you are floating an unfamiliar area, check out your planned trip with someone in the area after examining the maps or written discription. I recently reviewed the guidelines for a float trip that said that a short portage was needed around the west end of a certain dam. The writer, apparently having never floated this section himself, had neglected to mention that there was a sheer rock cliff over a hundred feet high on that end of the dam—which would make for a sporty portage.

One of the most productive methods of fishing from a canoe is for one person to handle it from the stern while his partner fishes from the bow. Rotating every half hour or so assures good fishing for you both. This tactic lets the angler in front concentrate on his fishing while his partner watches downstream to select the best fishing areas and maneuver the canoe into them.

Floating is an ideal way to fish surface bugs along banks, grassbeds and islands. The canoe is run parallel to the cover a comfortable casting distance out at about the speed of the current. This enables the angler to drop his bug close to the bank and get a nice long drift, since both the canoe and the bug are drifting downstream at about the same rate.

If your partner is reading the water and handling the canoe properly you can easily drop your bug into a different hot spot with each cast. The technique most often employed is to drop the bug right at the water's edge and fish it out only about ten feet before picking it up and casting to a new spot downstream.

When using this tactic it is best to cast the bug downstream about ten or fifteen feet ahead of the canoe. This gives you the most control of the bug action and the longest possible drift. The canoe will usually be going slightly faster than the bug since the current is slower at the edges of the stream. If the cast is made straight out, or slightly behind the canoe's position, you can end up with a dragging action on the bug.

Although many anglers feel river floating for smallmouth is at its best with surface bugs, there is nothing wrong with fishing streamers and nymphs from canoes. These can be fished along the banks and edge cover as just described, but they may actually out-produce the surface bugs in slow, deep water. Mid-pool stretches five to ten feet deep, with bottoms of boulders or sloping ledges, are definitely worth fishing. Here the canoe can be anchored while both anglers cover all of the water within reach before raising anchor to move downstream.

If the current is slow the canoe can drift on its own as both anglers fish. Usually the canoe turns across the current and you end up fishing in directions other than you planned. This is not as bad as it sounds—these big pools have good water in many directions.

A popular fly in this situation is a big Fur Leech fished right along the bottom. In some cases this can be handled with a floating line and a ten- to twelve-foot leader. If you can give it enough time, and the current is not too strong, a well weighted Fur Leech will usually pull this leader down. In some situations a sinking-tip line with a six-foot leader is more efficient. This gets the streamers to the bottom quickly and helps hold them there as you swim them around boulders and between ledges. Unfortunately there are no rules that can tell you when to switch over to the sinking-tip line. Basically it boils down to how well you are doing with the floating line. If you are not getting strikes or bumping the bottom when using the floater, it's time to switch to the sinking-tip line.

Nymphs can also be effective in this deep water, but remember that many nymphs, such as the hellgrammites and stoneflies, prefer well-aerated water in riffles. Thus you can expect your best action in the upper section of these pools.

A heavy emergence or spinner fall of mayflies, as discussed in the chapter on dry flies, can produce some outstanding action in these big pools. This does not occur every day, but when it does, the fishing is tremendous. Once you hit one of these hatches make a note on the calendar, because they will be on at about the same time next year.

Despite how great river canoe fishing can be, there are some negatives to own up to. Some people are not comfortable sitting down to fish all day, especially in a canoe with seats close to the floor. Before you decide to stand up in any boat or canoe to do your fishing, make sure your craft is stable enough to do this safely. Every year I hear stories from anglers who have toppled over in canoes. Many of them are purchasing replacement tackle.

Some canoes, especially those made of aluminum, can be very noisy which results in scaring fish. Shifting anchors, rolling rod cases, sliding ice chests, and even scuffing feet can generate strong sound vibrations through the water which alert the fish. This problem is worst in slow, shallow water but I have seen it hurt the fishing even in fast runs. Putting indoor–outdoor carpet on the floor helps. If the carpet is glued into place it is more secure, but keeping it clean can be a problem. If not glued into place it can be easily removed and hosed off.

When seated low in a boat or canoe some beginning anglers—as well as a few others—have trouble keeping their back casts from hitting the other fellow. A good friend who guides a lot of float trips can entertain you for a long time with stories about some of the unusual ways his clients have hooked him. Sounds funny, but it can be serious. For this reason, as well as simply keeping the back cast high for good control, many fishermen like fly rods that are at least nine feet long for canoe fishing.

11

Smallmouth in Lakes

There are many similarities between fly fishing for smallmouth bass in lakes and fishing in streams. Many of the same tactics and flies covered earlier work well in lakes, but a few additional aspects are worthy of consideration.

Seasonal effects upon the smallmouth require more attention in lakes than in streams, given the broader variety of water depths and locations from which the bass can choose. For example, when a river smallmouth gets the urge to spawn in the spring he may have to go only twenty feet to find an ideal depth with the correct bottom composition, whereas his cousin in a large lake may go quite a distance from where he spent the winter. In mid-summer, when the water gets hot, the river smallmouth can compensate only so much by seeking out deep pockets. The lake fish can head for the comfort of much deeper water—requiring anglers to adopt different tactics and tackle.

In the southern part of the smallmouth's range the action in lakes may start as early as March and good fishing can be expected as late as December. In the northern reaches things often do not get going well until May and slow down after October.

When fishing lakes it is essential to consider the composition of the bottom and general areas of cover. It would be easy to fish all day in water holding no smallmouth. One of the most consistent places to find fish are rocky areas—rocky drop-offs along the shore, sunken islands, shoals, rock piles, even man-made reefs. The mouths of feeder streams entering lakes are also worthwhile, especially when the lakes get warm, since most of these feeders are cooler than the lakes. Minnows, crawfish, and nymphs are often present in thick concentrations in these rocky areas and feeders.

The shade afforded by logs, overhangs, brush, sparse aquatic grass and even on-shore trees and shrubs provides additional appeal when found over bottoms

Charley Waterman used light fly tackle to take this nice smallmouth on a Maine lake. Photo by Charles F. Waterman.

of desirable composition. Often the shore line of a cove will produce best during that part of the day in which it has shade from the trees on shore. If this happens to be a shaded cove on the eastern side of a lake it will almost always provide better fishing early in the morning than it does in the evening—except in the early spring and late fall when the bass like the warmth the sun provides.

In the spring the smallmouth move into the shallows to prepare for spawning. This time yields some of the best surface action of the entire year. Some states and Canadian Provinces do not open their smallmouth season until after spawning takes place, so check before planning a trip into a new area. There is also an ongoing argument over the sportsmanship of fishing for smallmouth at spawning time, even if it is legal. This is a shot each angler must call for himself. On the positive side, under these conditions you know exactly where the bass are, and they are often easy to catch. The negative side is that we may be doing appreciable damage to future smallmouth populations. Certainly catching and killing a large female loaded with eggs will cost us a certain number of fish in the future.

Naturally the extent of this damage depends upon the number of spawning females being killed. There is some concern that smallmouth caught and even carefully released at this time of the year may not spawn as successfully as they would if left unmolested.

Most smallmouth fly fishermen return most fish and would not think of keeping a spawning bass. Many others refrain from fishing for smallmouth at all while the fish are on the spawning beds, choosing rather to fish for them just before or after spawning. Fish caught just prior to spawning season are always carefully released.

Beside spring, good action can be expected in the shallow areas of lakes in the fall and, on some lakes, throughout much of the season early in the morning and late in the evening. Many fishermen fish top-water patterns in the shallows as long as they are productive in the spring, since later in the summer they may be compelled to go deeper.

Working surface bugs on lakes is much like fishing them on streams, with

minor exceptions. If wind has created a fair amount of chop, floating bugs are not as productive as they are on quieter water. Sometimes imparting a lot of noisy action to the bug will make the bass come to it in rough water, but most of the time they don't know it's up there. Extra bug action can also be helpful if, all of a sudden, you find yourself fishing over deeper water and the action unexpectedly slows down. You have to get their attention.

The shallows can also be fished successfully with streamers. We are more concerned about the schooling minnows here, such as the shiners and shad-type minnows, than we are with the bottom huggers. Many of these minnows make their homes here all the time, and if you happen to be in a windward cove you can expect an additional supply. Casting a silverish streamer, such as Waterman's Silver Outcast or Trueblood's Black and White Bucktail, in close to the shore and stripping it back out usually does the job. If you are unable to identify any unusual features on the bottom you can systematically cover a broad area.

One day I was fishing one of these lakes and, by using polarized sunglasses,

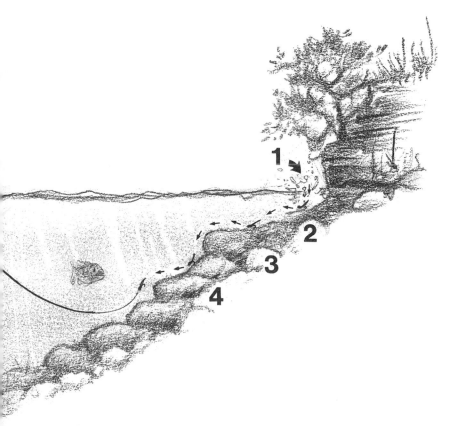

A sinking-tip fly line can be a big help in fishing the drop-offs in lakes. Cast a streamer close to the shore, then retrieve the fly with a darting action applied by the line hand. Allow enough time between each strip of the line for the fly to sink properly.

I was able to identify the tops of some huge boulders between the boat and the shore, even though they were in water twenty feet deep. I cast streamers in close to the shore and, though the water there was only several feet deep, I got no strikes until the flies approached the boulders. Almost every boulder produced several good fish.

When working streamers along shores, islands, and rock piles a floating fly line with a nine- to twelve-foot leader will usually work. On some occasions smallmouth are willing to come up through surprisingly deep water to take flies. If we need to get our flies down about five feet this can be achieved by selecting weighted streamers or by adding a size BB split shot to the leader. When more depth is needed, or if you want to fish your streamers with a slight diving or jigging action, you can use a mini-sinking-head as described in Chapter 1. Don't sell these simple devices short. I've been using them for almost twenty years with great success.

Sinking-tip fly lines are great when fishing these edges with streamers. Manufacturers build these lines to sink at various rates. By determining the amount of drop off and floor depth in the area you want to fish you can choose the appropriate sinking-tip line for the job at hand. I find the highest density sinking-tip lines to be the most useful. These lines are almost as easy to cast as the full floaters, and with a little experimenting you will be amazed at what you can achieve with them.

It is very important to use a short leader with these sinking-tip lines. Remember that the way they get flies to the bottom is to first sink themselves and then pull the fly down with them. The longer the leader the more it nullifies this effect. I never use leaders over six feet long with a sinking-tip line and in special situations may go to one as short as two feet.

When fishing a sinking-tip line it is important to give it time to sink to the bottom before starting the retrieve. Also think about how the line is affecting the fly action during the retrieve. For example, let's assume you are fishing a sharp drop-off from an island and you want to work your streamer right along the bottom all the way down. If you think of this as fishing along the face of a hill you can easily visualize how the line and fly must be handled.

Upon presentation the streamer is allowed to sink to the bottom, followed by a slow, deliberate stripping retrieve. The line is stripped only about six inches with the line hand while the rod point remains low, pointing at the line-water entry point. It is very important to allow a long enough pause after the stripping movement to permit the line to pull the fly back to the bottom. If the stripping action is too fast, or there is not enough sinking time allowed between the strips, the streamer will angle up toward you rather than working down the face of the drop-off.

As you continue this strip-pause-strip retrieve you must allow more time between strips in order for the fly to get back to the bottom. Remember, this water is getting deeper all the time and it is going to take longer for the sinking-tip line to pull the fly back to the bottom. Also, the closer you retrieve the streamer to the boat the greater the angle at which you are pulling it up off the bottom. Give it time and your patience will be rewarded.

Deeper water, down to thirty feet, is often best worked with a full sinking-head fly line. These have thirty feet of sinking line which really takes the fly to the bottom. Again, I prefer the high-density style so I don't have to wait all day for it to reach the bottom. It is still important to use a leader no longer than six feet in order to help the line hold the fly close to the bottom.

Underwater fly selection can be more demanding in lakes than in streams. Lakes lack the current to help move the fly and make it look alive. Also, we often find a very slow retrieve beneficial in lakes. Due to this last aspect the flies we select to fish in very deep water must be carefully selected.

Patterns must incorporate soft, breathable, alive-looking materials which can be made to look appealing to the bass with very little action. This calls for flies tied either with fur, ostrich herl, marabou, or very soft hackle. This type of fly wiggles convincingly even when retrieved at a slow pace. Flies that fall into this category include Eelworm streamers, Zonkers, Fur Leeches, Strymphs, Woolly Buggers, Flash-A-Buggers, and even Marabou Muddlers.

Since accurate determination of the smallmouth's location at these depths is difficult, many anglers like to use tactics that will attract the fish if they are a little off in fly placement. Since a fast action is seldom the best at these depths, a good compromise is a jigging-type action. This can be achieved by allowing the fly to sink all the way to the bottom on presentation, then with the line tight from the line hand all the way to the fly the rod tip is lifted sharply about two feet. The rod is then slowly dropped back to its original position. This action makes the fly dart up from the bottom and dive back. The rate of dive can be increased by using streamers with weighted heads or by adding a size BB shot to the leader immediately ahead of the fly.

As the fly sinks back to the bottom it is doing so on a slightly slack line. A strike at this point can be difficult to detect fast enough to set the hook on the fish. To compensate for this it is sometimes beneficial to strip in six to ten inches of the slack line with the line hand as you are dropping the rod. Be careful not to overdo this stripping; if excessive it will kill the jigging effect. Sometimes it is better to wait until the fly settles all the way to the bottom before stripping the line.

Another good streamer action in water down to twenty-five feet is the crawling-type retrieve. Here the fly is allowed to sink to the bottom and a steady retrieve is used—sometimes with hesitations of various lengths. The crawling action can be achieved with a steady, line-hand twisting retrieve or with a slow, steady line-hand stripping motion. With both methods I like to have the line pass over the index finger of my rod hand on the way up to the stripping guide. This provides an extra measure of control.

Weed guards are almost a must on these deeply fished flies in lakes. Admittedly they cost some missed strikes, but that's the price we pay for fishing deep. Many of these misses come from not setting the hook firmly on the strike.

There is nothing different about setting the hook on a fish in deep water—just do it with more gusto when the fish are deep. Use the line hand to strip-strike the fish at the same time you hit him with the rod. Raise the rod sharply with the whole arm—locking the wrist in line with the forearm in the process. This moves the whole rod and enables you to get the backbone of the rod butt into the strike. Moving the rod through a wide arch with the wrist only is a poor strike

and results in many missed fish. The wrist-only strike puts most of the load on the rod tip, which flexes against the resistance of the deeply sunken fly and heavy line and does not sink the hook into the bass.

One final note: avoid standing in a boat or canoe when fishing lakes. This high silhouette can scare the bass a considerable distance away, especially when fishing shallow water.

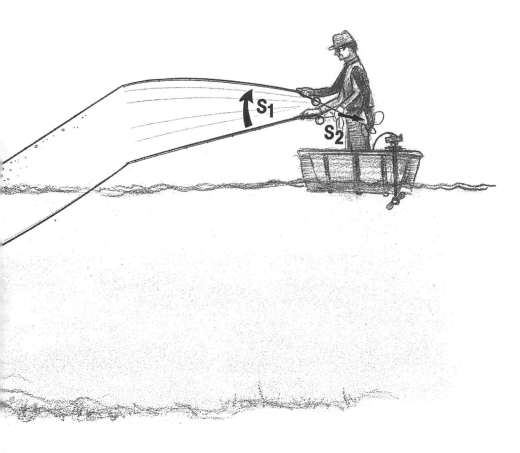

"There is nothing different about setting the hook on a fish in deep water—just do it with more gusto when the fish are deep." (S1) Raise the whole rod firmly while locking the wrist in line with the forearm, in order to take advantage of the stiff butt of the rod. (S2) Simultaneously, apply a strip-strike with the line hand.

12

Tying Smallmouth Flies and Bugs

Before selecting any fly, consider whether it can be made to fish properly in the situation you plan to encounter. This is the most significant feature considered by knowledgeable fly tyers as they design a new fly or change existing patterns.

There is something to be said for designing beautiful flies as an art, and all tyers enjoy constructing flies with exotic body parts that end up looking like the living counterpart. The trouble is they just don't fish well.

Poul Jorgensen, one of the worlds finest fly tyers and fishermen, recently presented a tying demonstration at a sportsmen's show. On request Poul tied a specific hard-body nymph using components that looked exactly like that body part on the real insect. Tails, feelers, wing pad, legs (with joints), exact body segments—all magnificently incorporated into a masterpiece fly. When the crowd thinned out, I asked Poul if he usually fished that pattern or his impressionistic fur version of the same insect. He looked up, first in surprise, and then sort of chuckled and replied, ''definitely the fur version.''

What enables a fly to fish properly? And how can we build this into our patterns?

In order to answer these questions we must examine how the food we are trying to imitate acts in or on the water. We must understand what we can expect of our own skills in handling the fly in the water. And we need an understanding of tying materials.

A perfect example is the hellgrammite fly pattern. Long ago we realized that conventional ties did not catch anything like the smallmouth that fell to the real hellgrammite used by bait fishermen. Seeking to find the answer I decided to see how the real larva acted in the water, and compare the results with the flies I had been using. Some hellgrammite flies, like those sold by Abercrombie

Catching large smallmouths consistently requires a variety of flies that can be fished in different ways to meet changing demands by the fish. Photo by Charles F. Waterman.

and Fitch in the early 60s, looked so much like the real thing you almost expected them to crawl out of your fly box. There had to be more to it than the look of the fly.

I collected real hellgrammites from the stream bottom and released them into the water where I could observe their actions. Some were released in fast water, some into shallow water and in a broad variety of currents.

When dropped into the stream a few rolled themselves into a tight ball and sank quickly to the bottom. However, the majority of them swam downstream with a pronounced undulating action as they gradually angled down toward the stream bottom.

It quickly became apparent why the flies I had been using were so disappointing. They all drifted through the water in a rigid, surfboard posture which never resembled the action of the real hellgrammite. To duplicate the undulating action of the naturals I tried many different styles of tie but none, not even the hinged-style wiggle-nymphs, were a great improvement.

About that time Ron Kommer and I were working on a series of king-size streamers with ostrich herl wings. We tried this herl on the hellgrammite, tying it in at the tail position. We considered it as an extension of the hellgrammite's body and kept it almost as full as the body. The rest of the fly was pretty standard, utilizing Charlie Brooks' ''in-the-round'' style of body and dark rubber pinchers.

This fly turned out to be more effective than we had ever hoped for. The ostrich herl solved our problems of duplicating the undulating swimming action of the real hellgrammite. When it became wet the strong stems of the herl had a great affinity for each other and adhered nicely together. Consequently when we fished this fly—which later became known as Murray's Hellgrammite— upstream dead drift it wiggled like the real thing. All of the other materials we had used in this extended-body style tie had collapsed when fished upstream if the fly was moving just slightly slower than the current. Marabou, for instance, when used in this manner collapsed down over the fly like a folded umberella. A Woolly Bugger for instance is a great fly when fished against or across the current, and even good fished upstream as long as it is retrieved faster than the current is returning it. However, if the current upstream pushes the marabou tail faster than you are retrieving the fly this material folds down over the fly in a very unnatural manner.

Developing flies is not a matter of making a profound discovery, nor is it luck. What's required is an understanding of the problem, knowing our fishing capabilities and the tying materials, and experimenting until a successful pattern is developed. Long ago I decided to see if I could learn one new thing every time I went fishing. It's been a helpful rule: some days nothing new presents itself, but at other times I observe several points about the fish, the fishing or the flies that I had been unaware of.

If you tie your own flies you have a fair amount of latitude in selecting materials to assure that your flies will fish properly. For example, if you are going to fish a bug on top you want to select as its primary component a good floating material—easy if you are tying hard-head bugs. It's simple to tell if the cork, balsa wood or plastic bodies do the job by first dropping them in the kitchen sink. Hair selection is another matter. Many writers have tried over and over again to tell us how to select the proper hair for surface bugs but the point is very difficult to make. Not one bug tyer in ten standing before the huge rack of hairs in my shop picks the appropriate patch for the job at hand. What you are looking for is strong, hollow hair but you can simplify your search by asking a competent salesman to help you.

Once you have selected the primary floating component for a surface bug —cork, balsa wood, hair, or what have you—don't counterbalance this with materials that will absorb water and sink the bug. Materials like soft hackle and marabou can enhance the bug's action, but don't overdo them.

Hook selection for surface bugs is crucial. Since we use larger bodies on these flies than we do on underwater flies, be sure you have enough space between the body of the bug and the point of the hook in order to hook the bass on the strike. There are two ways to achieve this: one is to select hooks that have a large gap (space between the point of the hook and the shank) in relation to their length. The other is to select 3X or 4X long-shank hooks in order to move the point away from the body of the bug. Be careful, though, since smallmouth hit toward the head of a fly or bug you can miss some strikes by using hooks with 6X or 8X long shanks.

The body size and shape of a surface bug also affect its hooking qualities. Cork and balsa bodies must not be too big for the hook size. Spun-hair bugs must be trimmed very close to the shank on the underside. Pull-over hair bodies, as in the Drake's Slider, must not be tied with enough hair to block the gap.

Weed guards can also slightly affect hooking. If you fish around lots of weeds or swim streamers right on the bottom you may not be able to get by without them. Experiment with guards of various stiffness and styles of ties so you have maximum control.

Hook selection is also important in underwater smallmouth flies. Excessively long hooks cause missed strikes here as well as on surface bugs, but a more common problem is too heavy a hook with large diameter wire. I was guilty of this long ago until a friend pointed out why I was missing strikes. It is logical to use heavy hooks to help sink nymphs and streamers, but the advantage gained does not begin to offset the number of missed strikes they cause. I see some bass flies tied on such stout hooks that their points look as large as a ball point pen's; you couldn't sink some of these into jello, let alone a smallmouth's hard jaw. We don't need to use extra-fine wire trout dry fly hooks on smallmouth flies, but the lighter the wire in the hook—up to the point of straightening on the strike —the more fish you will hook.

Mashing barbs down and keeping hooks sharp can also help improve our hooking rate. Several years ago we had about six weeks of truly outstanding fall fishing. It wasn't quite good enough that I was willing to see how many way-out tactics and flies would catch smallmouth, but it was good enough to prompt some experimentation. Having heard complaints about barbless hooks from fellows claiming they lost fish with them I decided to check this out as objectively as I could. I used the same patterns on barbed and barbless hooks, for equivalent time periods on water of equal quality. All fall I switched back and forth from barbed to barbless flies on every type water imaginable.

The result was that I landed almost thirty percent more fish per strike on barbless hooks than on barbed hooks. I lost *some* fish on the barbless hooks— but since I hooked a greater percentage of the fish on the strike with the barbless hooks, I was still way ahead of the game. If you have ever landed a bass and noticed that the hook has not penetrated beyond the barb you can see why barbless improves the catch. That bass in your hand had not been struck solidly enough to sink the barb, or maybe the hook struck him in a tough spot. For whatever reason he was one of the few you'll land in that manner; the others jumped or pulled off to freedom. You can't land many fish on the point of a hook.

When we strike the bass with a barbless hook there is no resistance to keep the hook from penetrating all the way to its bend. The bass pulls against the deep part of the hook, not just hanging on the hook point. You land more fish because you hook more fish—try it.

The sinking rate and action of underwater flies can be altered by the amount and location of lead added when tying the fly. One method of doing this is to wrap fuse-type lead wire onto the hook shank. This is done after under wrapping the shank with tying thread. Both are then coated with cement to assure a solid foundation for the main part of the fly.

This lead comes in a variety of diameters. The finer diameters are used on the smaller hooks, the larger on big hooks. In this way the sinking rate is controlled. The number of wraps used will also affect sinking rate. For example, in specific situations I have used a double-overlapping wrap of the largest lead on the whole length of some long-shank size 2 hooks. It casts like a cannon ball but it does get to the bottom in a hurry. The worst thing about flies with excessive weight like this is that they are almost dead in the water. Neither we nor the current can make them look very appealing to the fish.

I tie some of my favorite flies in three different weights to meet various demands. This is done by altering the amount of lead under the fly body. To pick the one needed from my fly box quickly I color-code them, tying each of three different weights with a different color thread.

Another system of altering the sinking rate and fly action is to add extra weight to the head area of the fly as it's tied. Bathtub chain eyes and lead barbell style eyes do a good job here. They are usually exposed in the final fly but can be partly hidden with dubbing or yarn if you feel they are too exaggerated. Weights in the head area of the fly are great for enhancing the jigging effect in leeches and some streamers. Naturally they can be added just above the bend of the hook if this would fill a specific need. Be careful not to close the gap area when using them here.

Thread for tying smallmouth flies should be in proportion to the job required. Many people break the thread when spinning the hair on surface bugs. This can be simplified by using size A monocord or Kevlar thread. In fact, there is nothing wrong with using these in a variety of flies, except that they build up quickly. Many tyers find that size 3/0 prewaxed monocord works very well on most flies. It has adequate strength, lies flat, and is very easy to work with.

The following selection of smallmouth flies, accompanied by brief tying instructions, is only a representative group that does include some outstanding, but little-known patterns. This is not intended to be a comprehensive section on fly tying. Many excellent pattern books are available which list a broad selection of flies with the various components used in each. Likewise there are numerous how-to-tie books available. I have also simply listed some productive smallmouth flies in their most popular sizes. These flies can be found in many general pattern books.

The order in which the flies are listed is roughly the way they are covered earlier in this book—starting with topwater patterns, followed by streamers and ending with nymphs.

In tying the following patterns I apply cement after each step to the tie-in and tie-off points, especially when adding new materials. I use flexament and place it in a 3cc hypo syringe so I can quickly add a drop or two where needed.

WHITLOCK'S HAIR GERBUBBLE BUG

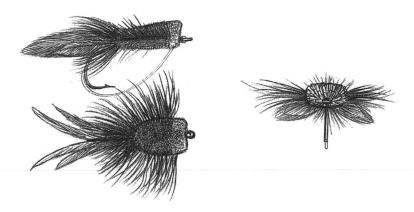

Hook: Mustad 37187 (stinger) size 6, 10; Mustad 94840 sizes 4 through 8
Thread: Kevlar or size A prewaxed monocord
Body: deer, elk, or antelope body hair (natural or dyed)
Wings: four large, soft, cock-neck hackles
Tail skirt: two soft, webby cock hackles
Weed guard: stiff nylon monofilament (.018 inch to .024 inch diameter)
Instructions: Attach the thread above the hook bend and tie in a three-inch piece of monofilament, flattened on the end, on top of the shank.

For the tail tie in two pairs of hackles about one half times the length of the hook shank over the mono so each pair flairs to the right and left of the shank. Form a tail skirt by tying and wrapping two neck hackles immediately in front of the tail. The barbules should be about one and a half times the hook's gap. Tie in two pairs of hackles on each side in front of skirt as wings with tips pointing to the rear. These should be twice the length of the shank and twice as wide as the gap.

Tie in and spin several bunches of hair to form the body in front of the wing tie-down point. Pack each bunch tightly against the previous bunch. Continue until all but one quarter of the shank behind the eyes is covered. Place two half hitches in front of the hair body and cut thread.

Remove the bug from the vise and trim to shape with a razor blade or scissors. Leave the sides flat in order to provide a good foundation for the wings.

Place the bug back in the vise and attach the thread where you left off. Working with each side wing separately, fold the hackle barbules so they are exposed only on the outside portion of the stems. Fold one wing forward so that it sinks into the side of the hair body right along the shank as deep as it will go. Tie this off in front of the hair, then pull the opposite wing forward in the same manner and tie it off. Trim off the hackle tips.

Add one or two more bunches of the same-color hair in front of the wings and pack them tightly. To aid in visibility add, flair, and pack one bunch of white or lightly colored hair in front of the last two.

Remove the bug from the vise and trim the head so it's in line with the rest of the body.

Return the bug to the vise and pass the monofilament through the vise jaws and up through the hook's eye. Hold this in place with tying thread and adjust the mono so it passes below and in front of the hook point about one quarter of an inch. Tie mono down tightly with thread and trim off excess mono. Whip finish head and apply cement.

After removing bug from vise add cement along the bug's belly in line with the hook shank.

HOMELY HAIR MOUSE

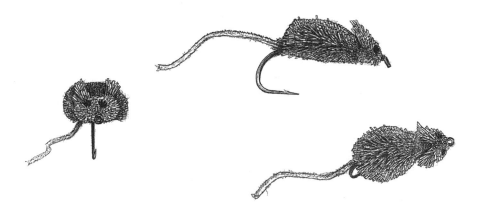

Hook: Mustad 9671, sizes 2 through 8
Thread: Kevlar or size A prewaxed monocord

Body: deer or elk body hair
Tail: chamois leather
Ears: same hair as the body
Eyes: black paint
Instructions: Tie in a piece of chamois leather about one-eighth to one-quarter of an inch wide, and the length of the hook shank on top of the hook, just in front of the bend to serve as the tail. Do not permit the tying thread to get very far up the hook shank ahead of the tail tie-in point. Hair bodies are much easier to spin on a clean hook shank without other materials, or even thread, to interfere.

Tie in and spin enough bunches of strong hair to reach to the eye of the hook. It is very important to clean all of the fuzz and short hair from each bunch of hair before spinning it. I find this easiest to achieve by holding the bunch by the tips after cutting it from the skin and brushing it firmly eight or ten times with a hard toothbrush. Cutting the hair tips before spinning can simplify the job.

Apply a whip finish behind the eye and remove the bug from the vise. Trim to the mouse shape with a razor blade or scissors. Be careful not to cut off the tail. Apply black paint for the eyes and the mouse is complete.

KRAZY KICKER FROG

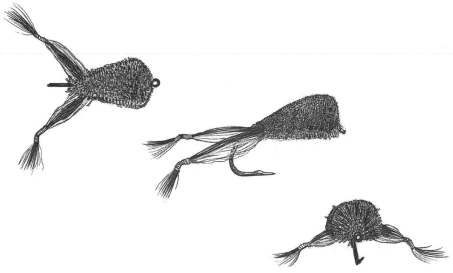

Hook: Mustad 3399A size 2 through 8
Thread: size A prewaxed monocord or Kevlar
Body: green deer hair
Legs: green and yellow bucktail
Instructions: Spin a small bunch of green deer hair at the rear of the hook shank to provide a wedge around which the legs will kick. Trim to shape.

Build the legs separately before applying them to the hook by using a small bunch of green bucktail over a small bunch of yellow bucktail about twice the length of the hook shank. Form the knee joint with a fine wire and over-wrap this solidly about a quarter of an inch with tying thread. Bend to desired angle. Saturate this joint with glue and allow to dry.

Tie in one leg at a time immediately in front of the hair wedge already on the hook. The yellow portion of the leg should be on the bottom side and it should be in a straight line with the hook shank and extend about one hook-shank length behind the bend. The end of the leg beyond the knee joint should point straight out from the center line of the bug. Tie the second leg in on the opposite side of the shank. The legs should be the same length, with the same amount of materials and point away from the body at the same angle. This makes the frog cast smoothly and prevents twisted leaders.

Continue adding and spinning enough green deer hair to reach the eye. Tie off with a whip finish and apply cement to the knot.

Remove the bug from the vise and trim to a frog shape using care not to cut the legs.

SHENANDOAH HAIR POPPER

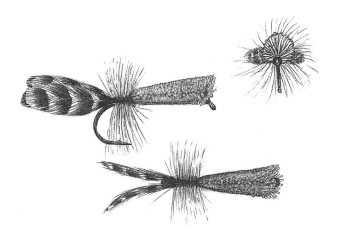

Hook: Mustad 9671 sizes 2 through 10
Thread: Kevlar or size A prewaxed monocord
Body: deer hair—black, yellow or green
Tail: wide hen saddle hackle-grizzly
Tail skirt: soft rooster saddle hackle-grizzly
Instructions: For the tail tie in two wide grizzly hen hackle tips with the shiny sides against each other so they flair slightly to opposite sides. Figure-eight these with tying thread to lock them into place.

Form the tail skirt by tying in and winding one or two soft rooster grizzly hackles immediately in front of the tail.

Tie in, spin, and tightly pack enough bunches of deer hair to reach the eye. Whip finish the head and apply cement.

Remove the bug from the vise and trim to a reverse-bullet shape with the large part toward the eye.

This is an excellent all-around bug. It can be tied in many colors and shapes. It can be trimmed closely for use on light rods. Saturate the face with several coats of flexament or epoxy and it pops quite well.

FLYING HAIR MOTH

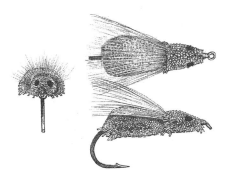

Hook: Mustad 9671 sizes 4 through 8
Thread: Kevlar or size A prewaxed monocord
Body: natural deer hair
Wing: white bucktail
Instructions: Beginning at the top of the hook bend tie in, spin, and tightly pack enough bunches of natural deer hair to reach two thirds of the way to the eye of the hook.

Tie off, apply two hitches, cut the thread, and remove the bug from the vise. Trim to a cylindrical shape and place the bug back in the vise and attach the thread right where you left off.

Form the wing by tying in enough white bucktail right in front of the deer hair to reach just beyond the bend of the hook. This wing should lie uniformly across the top of the deer hair body and angle up just slightly above it. Cut off the excess butts of the bucktail.

Tie on, spin and pack enough bunches of deer hair to reach the eye. Whip finish, cut the thread, and apply cement to the knot.

Remove the moth from the vise and trim the remaining deer hair in line with the rest of the body.

LEFTY'S POTOMAC RIVER POPPER

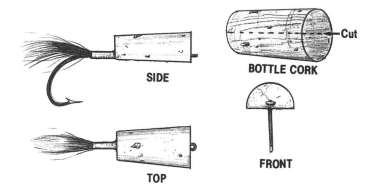

Hook: Mustad 33903 size 8 through 1
Thread: 3/0 monocord
Body: cork
Tail: squirrel tail
Paint: yellow
Instructions: Trim cork flat in front, back and along one-third of the belly. Taper cork from a large head to a slightly smaller rear area. Cut a groove along the underside to receive the hook. (Lefty uses a jig for this cutting process that greatly simplifies the job.)

Place the hook in the vise and form a full thread body to assure good cork-to-hook glue bonding. Tie in a short tail of squirrel tail at the rear of the hook shank. Coat the portion of the cork to receive the hook with epoxy. Clean the groove in the cork and apply epoxy. Place the cork onto the hook so it lies in a straight line with the bottom of the cork. Set this aside until it is completely dry.

Seal the cork and paint.

SMALLMOUTH CUPPED FACE CORK POPPER

Hook: Mustad 33903 size 1 through 8
Thread: size A or 3/0 prewaxed monocord
Body: cork
Tail: 3 pairs of soft rooster hackle
Tail skirt: soft rooster hackle
Instructions: Coat forward portion of hook shank with a thick layer of tying thread. Cover this portion of the hook with an overnight epoxy. Cut and clean the groove on the underside of the cork body and work epoxy into the groove with a dubbing needle; then insert hook. Place several wraps of thread over the cork. Remove this from the vise and allow to dry overnight.

The next day clean, seal and paint your bug the desired color.

Once the paint has dried place the hook in the vise and attach the tying thread behind the cork. For the tail select three pairs of soft, broad hackle feathers. Tie three in on each side of the shank with the shiny sides facing in. Figure-eight these with the tying thread to assure that they flair slightly outward. The finished tail should be about the length of the hook shank.

The tail skirt is tied between the tail and the cork body. For this select several soft hackle feathers with barbules about twice the length of the hook gap. Tie these in, wind them and tie them off right behind the cork. Apply a whip finish, cut the thread and cement.

WATERMAN'S SILVER OUTCAST

Hook: Mustad 9672 or Tiemco 5262 sizes 2 through 8
Wing: bucktail—white, blue and yellow
Thread: black 3/0 prewaxed monocord
Body: flat silver mylar tinsel
Wing topping: peacock herl
Instructions: Attach thread behind the eye and wrap the shank to bend and back to one-fourth inch behind eye. Tie in tinsel and wrap to the hook bend and back to the tie-in point. Tie off with thread and cut off excess tinsel.

Tie in a sparse wing of three layers of bucktail about one fourth of an inch behind the eye. This wing consists of white bucktail next to the hook shank, followed by yellow bucktail, and next blue bucktail. This three-part wing should lie smoothly along the top of the hook and be approximately one and one half to two times the length of the hook shank.

The wing topping, consisting of six to eight strands of peacock herl, is tied in immediately on top of the wing and is the same length as the wing.

Trim off the butt ends of the bucktail and herl at an angle sloping toward the eye of the hook. Build a neat head with the tying thread. Apply a whip finish and cement.

WHITLOCK'S MATUKA SCULPIN

Hook: Mustad 9672 or Tiemco TMC 5262 sizes 2 through 8
Thread: 3/0 prewaxed monocord
Body: yellowish cream blended fur
Wing: four soft webby cree-neck hackles, tinted golden brown or golden olive
Ribbing: gold oval tinsel
Gill: red wool dubbing
Pectoral fins: two fanlike breast feathers from body of hen mallard, prairie chicken or hen pheasant
Collar: deer hair—natural light dun-brown, tinted yellow, golden brown, or golden olive, and black or very dark brown
Head: same as collar
Weight: lead wire
Instructions: Place hook in vise and wrap lead wire about fifteen turns onto shank. Wire should be about the same diameter as the hook wire. Leave the front quarter of the hook bare.

Tie in gold oval tinsel at the rear of the hook shank and secure the exposed end in the material holder on the vise. Apply the fur dubbing to the tying thread and wind the body forward over the rear two thirds of the shank.

Tie in two matched pairs of soft webby hackle feathers immediately in front of body. These should be about twice the length of the hook shank. Cut off excess butts. Either cut off or moisten and pull the bottom hackle barbules from the bottom of the feathers up to the top for the length of the hook shank. Moisten and stroke all of the barbules over the shank so they stand up straight. Hold the hackles down flat on top of the body and wrap the oval tinsel forward through the barbules in neatly spaced turns up to the tie-in point. Tie off tinsel with thread and cut excess tinsel.

Add the matched pectoral fins on each side of the hook shank in front of the body so they curve away from the hook shank. Apply the red wool dubbing to the thread and wind a one-eighth inch wide gill immediately in front of the pectoral fins.

Form the collar on the bare portion of the shank just in front of the lead by attaching a small bunch of light yellow deer hair with two or three loose turns of thread with the tip pointing toward the bend of the hook. Tighten very slowly and allow the hair to roll under the shank as it flares. Hold and secure this with two or three tight turns of thread. This begins the "stacking" of the deer hair which will enable us to build a collar and head with the light color on the bottom and the dark color on top.

Select a bunch of golden-brown deer hair and hold it directly over the top of the shank securing it loosely with two wraps of thread. Hold this tight with your fingers so it won't move. Tighten and flair the hair. The tips of this and the yellow hair should not extend past the tips of the pectoral fins. Directly over the brown add a small bunch of black or dark brown deer hair which is slightly longer than the hair already in place. Follow the same procedure as with the lighter hairs but do not allow them to mix.

Move the thread forward of the hair. Pack the hair tightly by pushing it firmly toward the body by holding the shank firmly with one hand while pushing the hair with the thumb and index finger of the other. Secure this with several wraps of thread.

Repeat the stacking procedure with the three hair colors on the bare exposed shank to complete the head. This should end with a distinct shading going from light on the underside to dark on top. Pack this tight back against the collar. Whip finish off at the eye and cut thread.

Remove the fly from the vise and trim the deer hair with curved-blade scissors. Trim the bottom flat and wide with a few hair tips left to extend back to the body. The red wool should be allowed to show. Trim the sides flat, wide and oval to achieve a toad-shaped head. Allow the brown hair tips to extend back to the fins. The top of the head is cut short, allowing the black hair tips of the collar to extend back in a dorsal fin fashion.

When trimming is complete apply thinned rod varnish as a cement to the underside of the head, the eye and a small amount on top of the head in line with the hook shank.

SHENK'S BLACK SCULPIN

Hook: Mustad 9672 or Tiemco TMC 5262 sizes 2 through 8
Thread: size A black prewaxed monocord
Body: black rabbit fur
Tail: black marabou
Pectoral and dorsal fins: black deer hair
Head: black deer hair
Weight: lead wire

Instructions: Place the hook in the vise and cover the rear two-thirds with tying thread. Wrap lead wire, about the same diameter as the hook wire, over the thread wraps. Coat with cement.

Tie in a marabou tail which is about the length of the hook shank. Cut off excess marabou butts. Advance the tying thread to mid shank. Form a spinning loop about two inches long. Cut black rabbit fur from the hide and insert into the loop so the fur fibers remain perpendicular to the loop. Blended fur will not work for this purpose. Insert a spinning tool into the bottom of the loop and spin tightly so the fur is locked into the twisted thread. At this point the locked-in fur fibers must radiate out at right angles to the thread forming the loop. If they become trapped under each other and lie down flat you will not be able to form the full body desired on the finished fly.

Wrap this fur chenille—as Ed Shenk calls it—over the rear two-thirds of the shank. When done properly the fur should radiate out from the hook much like the deer hair does on a spun hair bug before it is trimmed.

Trim this fur body into a minnow body shape with scissors. Trim the stomach flat, the sides slightly fuller, and the top so it is full in the front and tapers down toward the tail.

Form the pectoral and dorsal fins with black deer hair. Cut a medium size bunch of deer hair from the hide and clean it thoroughly with a toothbrush. Hold this firmly in place on top of the hook with the tips extending to the hook point. Place two loose wraps of thread around the hair and the shank and pull straight down while holding it to prevent spinning. The hair tips should radiate back evenly from both sides and the top of the body. Advance the thread through the butts while holding the tips. Place three wraps of thread in front of the butts to set them up and hold them in place.

Tie in, spin and flair a bunch of black deer hair for the head immediately in front of the last bunch. This hair is permitted to work all around the hook in the conventional manner. Apply a whip finish, cut the thread and cement the windings.

Remove the fly from the vise and trim the head in a broad flat oval shape. Use care not to cut off that portion of the hair tip extending back over the body, which forms the fins.

SHENK'S WHITE STREAMER

Hook: Mustad 9672 or Tiemco TMC 5262 sizes 2 through 8
Thread: white or gray 3/0 prewaxed monocord
Body: white rabbit fur
Tail: white marabou
Weight: lead wire
Instructions: Place the hook in the vise and cover the entire shank with thread and coat it with cement. Wrap the middle three-fourths of the shank with lead wire and secure with thread. Coat this with cement.

Tie in a white marabou tail about the length of the hook shank. Secure this with tying thread and cut off the excess marabou butts.

Advance the tying thread to mid-shank. Form a full white fur body in the same manner used on the Shenk's Black Sculpin. The only difference is that you now use white fur and continue the body all the way to the eye of the hook.

Tie off, apply a whip finish and coat the knot with cement.

Trim the fur in the same basic minnow shaped wedged body as on the Black Sculpin.

FUR LEECH

Hook: Mustad 9672 or Tiemco TMC 5262 sizes 2 through 8
Thread: black 3/0 prewaxed monocord
Tail: strip of black rabbit fur
Body: strip of black rabbit fur
Weight: lead wire
Undertail: red flashabou

Instructions: Place the hook in the vise and cover the entire shank with thread. Apply cement to the thread and cover three-fourths of the mid hook shank with lead wire. Wrap the thread over the lead and coat it with cement.

Tie in eight or ten red flashabou fibers over the hook bend and allow them to extend one-quarter of an inch behind the bend. Select a strip of rabbit fur on the hide which is about one-eighth inch wide and three inches long to form the tail and body. Tie this in immediately over the hook bend. It should lie flat with the tail extending behind the bend about one-half to three-fourths the length of the hook shank.

Advance the thread to the eye and wind the strip of fur in adjacent wraps around the shank all the way up to the eye. Tie in securely here with the thread. Cut off the excess fur strip and apply a whip finish. Coat the head with cement.

JAMES WOOD BUCKTAIL

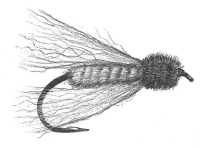

Hook: Mustad 94840 or 3906 size 2 and 4
Thread: black 3/0 prewaxed monocord
Wing: fine white bucktail
Rear body: yellow medium chenille
Forward body: blue medium chenille
Instructions: Tie in yellow chenille about one-quarter inch behind the eye of the hook and wrap it securely with the tying thread back to the bend. Advance the thread back to the tie-in point. Wind the chenille forward in adjacent wraps to the tie-in point and then back over itself about one-half of an inch and then back forward again to the starting point. Tie this off securely with the tying thread and cut off the excess chenille.

Tie in a sparse bunch of white bucktail right in front of the yellow chenille. The tips of the hair should extend about one-half inch beyond the bend and the entire bunch of hair should encircle the hook much like a wound hackle feather. Apply three snug wraps of thread over the hair tight against the chenille to encourage the hair to extend out slightly around the thick chenille wedge. This assures a pulsating swimming action. Cut off the excess hair butts.

Tie in a piece of blue chenille over the hair butts. Wind this forward to the eye and tie it off. Cut off excess chenille and apply a whip finish. Cement knot.

MURRAY'S HELLGRAMMITE

Hook: Mustad 9672 or Tiemco TMC 5262 sizes 4 through 10
Thread: black 3/0 prewaxed monocord
Body: black chenille
Extended body: black ostrich herl
Ribbing: soft dark blue dun rooster saddle hackle
Pinchers: black rubber
Weight: lead wire
Instructions: Place the hook in the vise and cover the entire hook shank with tying thread. Cover the middle three-fourths of the hook shank with adjacent wraps of lead wire about the diameter of the hook wire. Wrap the tying thread over this and apply cement.

Select strong ostrich herls with very thick hair-like side filaments for the extended rear body. (About twenty is right for a size 6 hook.) Holding the clump together break off the weak tips by twisting them between your thumbnail and index finger.

Tie the ostrich herl in just over the hook bend so the tips extend beyond the bend about twice the length of the hook shank. Tie the butts down along the top of the hook shank for two-thirds of its length to form a smooth underbody. Trim off excess butts.

Tie in a soft webby dark blue dun rooster saddle hackle over the bend by the tip. Tie in a piece of black chenille immediately over this. (The chenille must be in proportion to the hook size, but should be rather fat.)

Advance the thread to the hook eye and apply enough wraps here to cover the sharp edges of the eye and to form a flat foundation for the rubber pincers. About one-eighth inch behind the eye tie in a folded two-inch piece of medium size rubber fiber. Lock this into place with the thread and figure-eight each side so they stick out forward in line with the hook shank and spread apart at a 90-degree angle to each other. There should be enough space between the front of these pinchers and the eye of the hook to allow us to tie a Spence Turle knot here when attaching the fly to the leader. Hold both strands of rubber together and cut them even about three-quarters of an inch forward of the eye.

Wind the chenille forward, and tie off about one-quarter of an inch behind the eye. Cut off excess chenille. Wind the hackle forward with neatly spaced wraps and tie off in front of the chenille. (Use about five wraps on a size 6 Hellgrammite.)

Form a head with the tying thread and whip finish *behind* the rubber fibers. Apply cement to the head.

BITCH CREEK NYMPH

Hook: Mustad 9672 or Tiemco TMC 5262 sizes 2 through 8
Thread: black 3/0 prewaxed monocord
Body: black chenille
Forward underbelly: orange chenille
Hackle: soft brown rooster neck hackle
Tail and feelers: medium white rubber fibers
Instructions: Place the hook in the vise and cover the shank with tying thread. Apply cement. Wrap the middle three-fourths of the hook shank with lead wire about the same diameter of the hook shank. Wrap thread over this and apply cement.

Tie in a folded two-inch piece of medium size white rubber on top of the shank just over the bend of the hook. Lock this in place with the thread so each side of the tail is in line with the hook shank and spread apart at about a 90-degree angle to each other. Figure-eight these with the thread to hold them securely.

Tie in a piece of black chenille at the rear of the hook shank. Wind this over the rear two-thirds of the shank and place two wraps of thread over the last forward wrap. Do not cut off the chenille. Tie in a soft brown hackle feather which has barbules twice the length of the hook gap right in front of the chenille. Tie in a two-inch piece of orange chenille on the underneath side of the hook right in front of the black chenille.

Advance the thread to the eye and form a flat foundation for the feelers. Tie in a two-inch piece of medium white rubber on the flat part of the shank about one-eighth of an inch behind the eye. Divide these and lock them into place the same way you did the tail except have these tips going out beyond the eye of the hook.

Wind the black chenille forward, tie off behind feelers and cut off excess. Pull the orange chenille forward along the stomach of the fly and secure it with the thread at the same place the black chenille stopped. Cut off excess chenille. Wrap the hackle forward in five or six neatly spaced turns and tie this off just ahead of the chenille. Form a neat head with the thread and apply a whip finish *behind* the rubber feelers. Apply cement to the head.

Cut the rubber tails and feelers to about one-half to three-quarters of an inch long.

BROOKS' DARK STONEFLY NYMPH

Hook: Mustad 9672 sizes 4 through 8
Thread: black 3/0 prewaxed monocord
Body: black fuzzy yarn
Hackle: one grizzly saddle and one grizzly dyed dark brown
Tail: six fibers of raven or crow primary
Gills: light gray or white ostrich herl
Rib: copper wire
Instructions: There is some latitude in tying this pattern, but these are Charlie's directions:

Cover hook shank with thread and coat with cement. Wrap most of hook shank with large lead wire and overwrap with thread. Cover with cement.

Tie in tail fibers and split them so three fibers are on each side. Tie in rib and yarn. Wind thread forward, half hitch twice and cut off.

Wind yarn to eye, back to the bend, forward to the eye, and back to the base of the thorax. Tie in thread at this point and tie off yarn. Wind rib and tie off.

Tie in a strand of ostrich herl and both hackles by the butts. Strip fibers from the lower side of each hackle. Wind two separated turns of hackle, one at the base of the thorax and one half way between there and the eye. Both colors of hackle should lie adjacent to each other. Tie off. Wind the ostrich herl forward at the base of the hackles and tie this off. Wind the thread forward and build a large head. Coat with cement.

STRYMPH

Hook: Mustad 9672 or Tiemco TMC 5262 sizes 2 through 8
Thread: 3/0 prewaxed monocord, color to match body
Body: black, cream, or olive rabbit fur
Tail: ostrich herl to match body
Collar: speckled Indian hen saddle hackle
Weight: lead wire
Instructions: Place the hook in the vise and cover the whole shank with thread. Coat with cement and wrap lead wire of the same diameter as the hook wire over three-fourths of shank. Overwrap with thread and coat with cement.

Select a bunch of strong ostrich herl with thick, full side filaments for the tail (about twenty on a size 6 hook). Break off the weak tips with your thumb and index finger. Tie these onto the top of the hook shank just above the bend. Cut off the excess butts. The tail should be about the same length as the hook shank.

Wind the thread to mid shank and form a two-inch-long spinning loop. Hook the spinning tool into the bottom of the loop. Cut the rabbit fur from the hide. Handle it carefully with a minimum of changing hands so you can insert this into the spinning loop perpendicular to the thread. Spin the loop, being sure to keep the ends of the fur sticking out to the sides of the loop so that only the central portions of the fur fibers become locked within the twisted threads. Be sure not to have fur within the upper half inch of the loop.

Wind the clear portion of the loop to the bend of the hook. Next wind the fur-filled loop in adjacent wraps to one-eighth of an inch behind the eye of the hook. Secure with tying thread and cut off excess.

Trim the fur body into a general minnow shape—flat on the bottom, fuller on the sides and longer on the top, which slopes from a fat head to a slimmer body where it meets the ostrich herl.

Tie in a speckled Indian hen saddle feather in front of the body, wind only two turns and tie off. Cut off the excess hackle tip, shape head and apply a whip finish. Coat head with cement.

These three basic shades—black, cream, and olive—were the first three I developed, but by utilizing the same materials in other colors, such as gray and dark brown, you can expand the usefulness of this pattern. The tail and body should be the same shade and the hackle should blend with these.

CRAWFISH

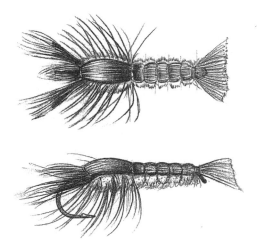

Hook: 9672 or Tiemco TMC 5262 sizes 2 through 8
Thread: 3/0 prewaxed monocord
Shell: fox squirrel tail
Pinchers: fox squirrel tail
Body: chenille
Rib: soft rooster neck hackle and size A monocord
Tail: fox squirrel tail
Weight: lead wire
Instructions: Place the hook in the vise and cover shank with thread. Wind lead wire over whole shank and apply cement. Overwrap with thread. Form the pincers by tying in a group of fox squirrel tail fibers by the tips just above the bend. Split these apart at a slight angle and lock into place with the tying thread.

Select a second bunch of fox squirrel tail hairs for the shell and tail and tie them in by the tips where the pincers are tied in. The butts of this hair should extend beyond the bend of the hook and be about one inch longer than the shank.

Tie in the chenille for the body and the hackle for ribbing over the squirrel tail. Wind the chenille over the rear one-third of the shank and tie off but do not cut. Wind the hackle forward in about three or four evenly spaced wraps over the rear one-third of the shank. Tie off the hackle and cut off the excess tip. Tie in a three-inch length of size A monocord at this point and hook into the material holder to use later as ribbing.

Advance the tying thread to the eye. Wind the chenille forward and tie off behind the eye. Cut off extra chenille. Pull the squirrel hair shell forward and place three wraps of tying thread over this just behind the eye.

Place two wraps of the size A monocord just in front of the hackle and wind this forward to the eye in evenly spaced wraps as ribbing to hold the shell in place. Tie off behind the eye and cut excess. Apply a whip finish knot behind the eye. Cut the thread and apply cement. Cut off the butts of the squirrel tail about one-fourth to one-half inch forward of the eye to form the tail of the crawfish.

By altering the colors of the materials from tan to brown to olive you can adjust this pattern to specific conditions.

SMALLMOUTH FLIES

TOP WATER

Patterns	Sizes
Tapply's Hair Bass Bug	2 through 6
Whitlock's Near Nuff Frog	2, 6, 10 (Mustad's stinger)
Krazy Kicker Frog	4, 6
Whitlock's Wigglelegs Frog	2, 6 (Mustad's stinger)
Whitlock's Mouserat	6 (Mustad's stinger)
Shenandoah Homely Hair Mouse	4, 6
Shenandoah Flying Hair Moth	4, 6
Spent Damsel-Dragon	6, 10 (Mustad's stinger)
Shenandoah Hair Popper	2 through 10
Whitlock's Most Hair Bug	2, 6, 10 (Mustad's stinger)
Whitlock's Hair Gerbubble Bug	2, 6, 10 (Mustad's stinger)
Dahlberg's Diving Bug	2, 6, 10 (Mustad's stinger)
Dahlberg's Diving Minnows	4, 8
Floating Muddler	2 through 8
Dahlberg's Rabbit Strip Divers	2 through 6
Jet Bug	2 through 6
Drake's Slider	1 through 6
Caddis Buck	6 through 10
Improved Sofa Pillow	6, 8
Improved Golden Stone	6, 8
Irresistible	8 through 12
Brown Drake	8 through 12
Elk Hair Caddis	8 through 12
Shenk's Cricket	8 through 12
Dave's Hopper	8 through 12
Shenk's Letort Hopper	8 through 12
Light Goofus Bug	8 through 12
Buck Bug	6 through 10
White Wulff	6 through 10
Lefty's Potomac River Popper	2 through 6
Gallasch Crawl 'N Twitch	4, 8
Gallasch Pop 'N Crawl	1, 4

Patterns	Sizes
Gallasch Spoutter Bug	1
Walt's Cork Poppers	2, 6
Sneaky Pete Popper	4, 8
Skipping Bug	1 through 4
Feather Minnow	2 through 6
Mississippi Bass Bug	2, 4
Gerbubble Bug	2, 4
Jorgensen's Balsa Popping Frog	2, 4
Gaines Popper	2 through 6
Peckinpaugh Popper	2 through 6

STREAMERS

Patterns	Sizes
Whitlock's Hare Water Pup	4
Fur Leech	2 through 8
Murray's Strymph	2 through 8
Woolly Bugger	2 through 8
Flash-A-Bugger	2 through 8
Whitlock's Sculpin	2 through 8
Shenk's Sculpin	2 through 8
Zonker	2 through 8
Spuddler	2 through 8
Whitlock's Prismatic Streamer	2 through 6
Muddler	2 through 6
Marabou Muddler	2 through 6
Shenk's White Streamer	2 through 6
Waterman's Silver Outcast	2 through 6
James Wood Bucktail	2 through 6
Lefty's Flash-A-Bou Streamer	2 through 8
Black Nose Dace	2 through 8
Marabou Streamer	2 through 8
Gray Ghost	2 through 8
Mickey Finn	2 through 8
Dark Spruce	2 through 6
Olive Matuka	2 through 6
Crawfish	2 through 6
Intergradation Bucktail	2 through 6
Light Edson Tiger	2 through 6

Patterns	Sizes
Whitlock's Chamois Leech	2 through 6
Dahlberg's Flashdancer	1, 4, 8
Whitlock's Eelworm Streamer	2 through 6
Whitlock's Multicolor Muddler	2 through 6

NYMPHS

Patterns	Sizes
Murray's Hellgrammite	4 through 10
Bitch Creek Nymph	4 through 8
Brooks' Dark Stone Nymph	4 through 8
Casual Dress	2 through 8
Damselfly Nymph	6 through 10
Dragonfly Nymph	6 through 10
Whitlock's Squirrel Nymph	6 through 10
Ted's Stonefly	4 through 8
Girdle Bug	4 through 8
George's Rubber Leg Brown Stone	4 through 8
Yuk Bug	4 through 8
Kaufmann's Simulator	4 through 8
Woolly Worm	4 through 8
Jacklin's March Brown Nymph	6 through 10
G. R. Hare's Ear Nymph	6 through 10
White Miller Nymph	8, 10
Murray's Strymph	2 through 8
Fledermouse	4 through 8

13

The Final Act

You did it. You finally caught that big smallmouth that has been outsmarting you all summer. Since that time last spring, when he broke you off after taking your fly in front of the log jam he calls home, you've had an ongoing one-on-one contest with him.

Somewhere along the line you even named him. He was often willing to swing out to investigate your offerings only to swerve away refusing them at the last instant. This bold turn often presented the big broad side of his body to you showing a flash of reflected light as he headed back home. Hence the name Flash.

Other than today and the time he broke you off, you only got the hook into him once, for just a split-second before he jumped and threw the fly. The other eight or ten trips when you tried him he was too smart for you.

Now that you are standing there in the water holding him by the lip as you remove your fly, what are you going to do with him?

You could take him home and have him for dinner, you could have him mounted for the office wall, or you could release him gently back into the river.

You are not really a selfish person but you consider all these possibilities carefully. Broiled with a little butter and lemon sauce he would make a fine dinner—but that would be a short-lived reward. If you had him mounted and put on the office wall you could tell stories of encounters with him to your fishing pals.

But would either of these be the greatest reward this bass could give? Reflecting upon the excitement he has given you over the months, think about what pleasures you could derive from future confrontations. Although he was smart before, he would be even tougher to catch in the future. Since he has already had a good look at all of the flies in your vest you may have to come up with some new, more convincing patterns. He just could be too tough to catch again!

So, what are you going to do with him? You make the call.

You did it! You finally caught the one that had been outwitting you. What's your next move? Wouldn't it be fun to catch him again some day—when you're both a bit older and wiser?

Index

Note: page numbers in italics refer to illustrations.

Murray's Fishing Shop
Edinburgh Va
fly fishing expert
No. Fork
said John y Downriver
Canoe on No fork